Apartheid and Racism in South African Children's Literature, 1985–1995

CHILDREN'S LITERATURE AND CULTURE

JACK ZIPES, SERIES EDITOR

Apartheid and Racism in South African Children's Literature, 1985–1995

Donnarae MacCann and
Yulisa Amadu Maddy

Routledge
New York & London

Published in 2001 by
Routledge
29 West 35th Street
New York, NY 10001

Published in Great Britain by
Routledge
11 New Fetter Lane
London EC4P 4EE

Routledge is an imprint of the Taylor & Francis Group.
Copyright © 2001 by Donnarae MacCann and Yulisa Amadu Maddy

10 9 8 7 6 5 4 3 2 1

Library of Congress Cataloging-in-Publication Data

MacCann, Donnarae.
    Apartheid and racism in South African children's literature, 1985–1995 / by Donnarae MacCann and Yulisa Amadu Maddy.
       p. cm. -- (Children's literature and culture ; v. 15)
    Includes bibliographical references (p.) and index.
    ISBN 0-415-93638-1 (alk. paper)
      1. Children's stories, South African (English)--History and criticism. 2. Children--Books and reading--South Africa. 3. South Africa--In literature. 4. Apartheid in literature. 5. Racism in literature. 6. Race in literature. I. Maddy, Yulisa Amadu, 1936- II. Title. III. Children's literature and culture (Routledge (Firm)) ; v. 15.

PR9362.6.C45 M34 2001
823'.91409358--dc21
                                      2001019461

Printed on acid-free, 250-year-life paper.
Manufactured in the United States of America.

Contents

*To the brave children who
have lost their lives in the
war against Apartheid.*

A Note about Terminology

The South African population was divided by the colonizing powers into the following broad categories: African, Asian (Indian), "Colored," and White. The Black Consciousness Movement in the late 1960s and early 1970s went a long way in uniting the first three groups into a political bloc. As South Africa's oppressed peoples, they adopted the term "Blacks." We are sometimes referring to this group collectively when we use this term. But the enslaved and colonized peoples were often treated by the ruling government as separate entities in a divide-and-conquer strategy. Thus in their book *Surplus People*, Laurine Platsky and Cherryl Walker refer to a distinct hierarchy within the Black group. They note that "the government takes into account who is being relocated and . . . what facilities it is going to lay on in any particular site. Coloured and Indian people are favoured over African, urban people over rural . . ." (1985, 338–339). According to these writers, "this corresponds to the divisions that [the Apartheid government] is trying to reinforce within the black population at every point" (1985, 339).

In children's literature, the groups featured are typically African, "Colored," and White. (South African Indians are rarely present.) We will use the term "Colored" (or "Coloured")—meaning people of mixed ancestry—for the sake of clarity. But this is the colonizer's invention and we will use quotation marks with this word. For the African group, we will use the terms African, indigenous African or people, and Black interchangeably. For Whites we will use the terms White South African, Euro-South African, Europeans, or simply White. But this group is also divided between Afrikaners (i.e., Boers, people of Dutch descent) and people of English descent, and sometimes this distinction is pertinent to the subject under discussion. We will capitalize the terms White and Black when they imply an ethnic population, but when there is a general color line connotation (as in "white supremacy"), a lower case letter will be used.

In quoting from South African publications, we will be repeating such terms as "Kaffir," "Bantu," "Hottentot," "Bushmen," and "Natives." But these are colonizer's names ("Hottentot" referring to the Khoikhoi people and "Bushmen" referring to the San people), and we will use quotation marks to indicate their foreign and pejorative origins.

Apartheid rule included the elaborate division of people for the sake of manipulation and control. This system required, therefore, a naming system that would make clear the different divisions and their slot in the social hierarchy. In children's books published in South Africa, a foreknowledge of this system is assumed.

WORK CITED

Platzky, Laurine and Cherryl Walker. 1985 (for the Surplus People Project). *The Surplus People: Forced Removals in South Africa*. Johannesburg: Ravan Press.

Preface

In 1996 we completed a study entitled *African Images in Juvenile Literature: Commentaries on Neocolonialist Fiction*, and we knew then that a more comprehensive study of South Africa was needed. Even though the findings of the South African Truth and Reconciliation Commission were not yet reported in the American press, it was clear to us that the South African situation was unique, its influence in Africa was unique, and its influence in the world was threatening. The Commission's revelations have reinforced that view, but the children's narratives that we covered in *African Images in Juvenile Literature* were enough to indicate that the Apartheid mindset would undoubtedly continue well into the twenty-first century.

Studies of the Apartheid ideology and regime, and in particular studies that show the indoctrination of the young, are a valuable predictive gauge for historians, policy makers, and the citizenry at large. Children's literature is a transparent window on the future—a way to glimpse how the literary imagination constructs cultural value. One important construct, the centuries-old white supremacist mythology, can be readily documented by way of stories conceived for the young.

South African experience is especially instructive because prejudice against blackness not only is frankly proclaimed in political organizations but also has a longstanding place in the educational system. Unless it is challenged at this institutional level, its influence on South Africans (and indeed on the larger world) can be exceedingly stubborn. In gauging that resistance to reform, we confine our study here to novels published in the decade surrounding Nelson Mandela's release from prison (1985–1995) since Apartheid's continuity over this period, rather than its decline, is so highly visible. A tenaciously white supremacist pattern dominates the storytelling. That is, Blacks are seldom endowed with full humanhood. They are targeted as a people with no history, a people frozen in time, a people incapable of progressive development.

Drawing upon his background as a historian, Basil Davidson (1972) refutes that spurious, ahistorical profile of Africans. He writes:

> [A]ll the peoples of Africa are in fact the product of an extremely long process of development. . . . In terms of their own history, they are very obviously developed peoples. They can be seen as "underdeveloped" only in terms of the quite different history of other peoples, whose own development has emerged and taken shape in quite different circumstances. (233)

Generally speaking, Davidson's understanding of "different histories" has yet to penetrate the children's book establishment of South Africa. This fact speaks for itself in the South African novels for children and young people.

WORKS CITED

Davidson, Basil. 1972. "Africa Recolonized?" In *Amistad 2*, eds. John A. Williams and Charles F. Harris, 229–260. New York: Vintage Books.

Maddy, Yulissa Amadu and Donnarae MacCann. 1996. *African Images in Juvenile Literature: Commentaries on Neocolonialist Fiction.* Jefferson, NC, and London: McFarland and Co.

Truth and Reconciliation Commission. 1999. *Truth and Reconciliation Commission of South Africa Report.* Vol. 1–5. London: Macmillan Reference Ltd.; New York: Grove's Dictionaries Inc.

Introduction

I have cherished the ideal of a democratic
and free society in which all persons live
together in harmony with equal opportunities.

—*Nelson Mandela, 1963*

S outh African children's novels (for ages eight to eighteen, approximately) have not portrayed Blacks as ready for "equal opportunities." Nor have they shown Africans capable of taking their destiny into their own hands. On the contrary, they have typically depicted them as entirely unfit for civic responsibility. The reasons for this Eurocentric approach reach back into colonial and neocolonial history. Children's literature is an indicator that points to the tenacity of such calculated racial bias. Although the turn-around in South Africa after the 1994 election was momentous, it was also limited, as Mandela (1995) cautioned his compatriots to understand: "We are not yet free; we have merely achieved . . . the right not to be oppressed." The follow up would be an "even more difficult road" (624). Similarly the Brookings Institute reported: "[Apartheid] as a way of life . . . will prove tenacious. So will the racism apartheid nurtured. . . [As] a formal model [apartheid] will end; apartheid as a mental and social model will persist" (Ohlson 1994, 185).

As the perpetrators of Apartheid crimes have received amnesty and walked away free, so the old educational system (and children's literature in particular) remains free to keep to its white supremacist path.[1] No viable educational policy serving all children was put in place for the "transition-to-power" years. Here we see a parallel between the direction taken in government and education that is not surprising. In his essay "What Can Become of South Africa?" Conor Cruise O'Brien (1987) comments on the culpability of educators:

Intellectuals, mainly teachers and *Predikants* [Calvinist clergymen],

were the originators and disseminators of Afrikaner nationalism, the
politico-cultural movement that eventually produced the doctrine and
system of Apartheid. . . . And it was also intellectuals who shaped and
refined that doctrine and system. (447)

The role played by the *Predikants* is more or less consistent with
Western church history in Africa. The imperialist colonization of
almost all of Africa was sanctioned by the church and blessed by its
bishoprics, as was the slave trade. In the same vein, Apartheid was the
work of intellectuals, educators, and church leaders, as well as business people and political operatives. South African children's literature
is an integral part of this broad, white supremacist program.

The question is not simply, "What can become of South Africa?"
There is an additional problem: "What have they done to the children?" Young people have learned to live in and with segregation, to
live apart from their parents, to grow up in barren "homelands" far
away from their rightful community of birth. They have lived with
hate and seen death stare them in the face through the barrel of a gun.
Children were in the forefront of the struggle that brought Nelson
Mandela into office as the first African president of South Africa. It
was the children, as O'Brien (1987) notes,

who made life impossible, often literally, for the agents of white
power in black townships. It is the children who enforce the boycotts,
whether of schools or of white shops. It is the children who discipline
those who are seen to step out of line . . . (431)

What hope have these children, most of whom have little or no education? What future have these children in a world where technology
holds the key to the future and this technology belongs to the White
managers? What hope is traceable even in the stories written after
Mandela's release in 1990?

A conservative, pro-Apartheid voice was active in children's book
publishing prior to the democratic elections of 1994, and that conservative presence is proving to be difficult to displace in the post-election
era. As essays in this collection reveal, a white supremacist theme continues, despite discernible anti-racist motives in works from the late
'80s and early '90s. Perhaps this is to be expected, since the whole educational system has been deprived of a democratic foundation, and re-
building will take time. The problem was only intensified when

African interests were not adequately protected in the compromises leading to the 1994 elections. In particular, in the negotiations to end white rule, the African National Congress (ANC) was not able to require the removal of White personnel in the civil and security services. This has resulted in persistent political destabilization at the institutional level.[2] In the field of literature, the old guard writers either resist change or fantasize that democratic reform has been instantaneously achieved, even while their own storytelling contradicts this fact.

White educators in particular have called for gradualism in educational change and for a "positive" approach in teaching the colonialist literature of the past. Such educators would keep Rider Haggard's (1885) *King Solomon's Mines* in the curriculum and teach it in a more "liberal," "positive" manner, but is such a strategy really "positive"? In the Western world, practically every European "classic" enjoys a sacrosanct status. Thus Rider Haggard's version of the white supremacy myth and the recent works that prolong Haggard's viewpoint remain essentially unchallenged. This conservatism remains intact, since the politically empowered group can almost always enforce its own prominent position within a colonial system; it can always require of the unempowered that they remain exactly where the colonizer positions them. The paternalism that tinged some imperialist beliefs made them seem benign to the colonizer, but not to the colonized.

The exiled Black writer Richard Rive (1988) pinpoints features of the "liberal" position in his discussion of South African novelist Olive Schreiner—features that are also traceable in much post-Apartheid educational thinking. Rive writes:

> [Schreiner] set the tone for white, liberal literature; an attitude that favoured non-revolutionay progress and reform for blacks. This implied a freedom of any individual to act or express himself in a manner of his own choosing, as long as this did not overtly challenge the white, civilised power structure. Liberalism in literature proved then, as it did later, to be writing by concerned white citizens read by other, sympathetic white citizens, about their moral, social and political responsibility towards blacks. There was concern spiced with trusteeship and more than a sprinkling of condescension. Although critical of racial discrimination, it saw the need for benevolent guardianship and understanding from a removed level. (199)

What Rive calls "condescension," "guardianship," and "understanding from a removed level" are qualities glaringly present in novels for the young. Moreover, most children's books are by "concerned White citizens" and are meant to be read by other White citizens. While the "liberal" children's writers strive for artistry, they are also striving for clarity about their continuing guardianship over social change. They want no mistaken interpretations. In their efforts to preserve the "civilized power structure," they express a mixture of fear and hostility toward Blacks. The intended anti-discrimination message is largely smothered by this anxiety, and it is likely that readers will come away viewing democracy not as a South African ideal, but as an essentially risky policy.

We can probe this ambivalence about democracy if we examine some of the major tenets of Apartheid. "Scientific" and theocratic forms of racism have been contrived by biologists and theologians, and it is instructive to study children's literature in this context. The relationship between racism and the dynamics of colonial rule is relevant. For example, children's books refer explicitly to the management of the labor pool, the management of residential segregation, and the practices of the police.

In Part 1 we take up the most essential social and political background information. We do not attempt a thorough overview of Apartheid history, but only those aspects that have been fundamental to the South African child's indoctrination. We explore those tenets of science, theology, and government that children have been taught as a prelude to their commitment to the doctrine of race hierarchy. Evidence that these subjects are foundational is in the stories themselves. Shake down any assortment of contemporary South African children's novels and a residue of South African assumptions will surface about science, theology, and government.

In Chapter One we cover the pseudo-science that has been one of Apartheid's basic building blocks. We examine the theology that posits Whites as a "chosen people" and the rightful overseers of Blacks and pinpoint the government policies and extra-constitutional arrangements that bring such myths close to daily experience.

Chapter Two highlights the "gatekeeping" in children's literature institutions (in libraries, schools, book selection committees, prize-awarding juries, the children's book press, the publishing industry, etc.). As South African literature has reflected the doctrines of Apartheid, so the work of educators and book critics has reflected these doctrines. Literary criticism, like other facets of the book world, has its agenda, and tends to support or refute the traditions of colonial domination.

In Parts 2 and 3 we cover novels with contemporary and historical settings, respectively. We examine the literary manifestations of pseudo-biology, colonialist paternalism, and repressive government. These broad themes take form in varied genres and settings. The specifics of a White imagination are traceable throughout the Western world, but this imagination is especially transparent in such an overheated context as South Africa—a nation struggling over issues of power and possession. In *Playing in the Dark: Whiteness and the Literary Imagination*, Toni Morrison (1993) speculates about the literary uses of a "color line":

> When does racial "unconsciousness" or awareness of race enrich interpretive language, and when does it impoverish it? . . . How is "literary-whiteness" and "literary blackness" made, and what is the consequence of that construction? (xii)

Her comment about the United States could be applied to South Africa as well: "Living in a nation of people who *decided* that their world view would combine agendas for individual freedom *and* mechanisms for devastating racial oppression presents a singular landscape for a writer" (xiii). This national irony finds its way repeatedly in South African novels geared toward the young.

Multicultural societies have a unique potential for embracing a philosophy of equality and mutuality. Children in particular have every reason to cherish their diversity, given the chance. This proverb from Congo (formerly Zaire) makes the case:

> Let the elephant fell the trees, let the bushpig dig the holes, let the mason wasp fill in the walls, let the giraffe put up the roof, then we'll have a house. (Knappert 1989, 27)

WORKS CITED

Haggard, Rider. [1885] 1958. *King Solomon's Mines*. Reprint, Harmondsworth, Middlesex, UK: Penguin Books.

Knappert, Jan. 1989. *The A–Z of African Proverbs*. London: Karnak House.

Mandela, Nelson. [1994] 1995. *Long Walk to Freedom: the Autobiography of Nelson Mandela*. Boston: Back Bay Books.

Morrison, Toni. [1992] 1993. *Playing in the Dark: Whiteness and the Literary Imagination*. Reprint, New York: Vintage Books.

O'Brien, Conor Cruise. 1987. "What Can Become of South Africa?" In *The Anti-Apartheid Reader*, ed. David Mermelstein, 430–473. New York: Grove Press.

Ohlson, Thomas, Stephen John Stedman, with Robert Davies. 1994. *The New Is Not Yet Born: Conflict Resolution in South Africa*. Washington, DC: Brookings Institution.

Rive, Richard. 1988. "The Black Writer and South African Literature." In *Towards Understanding: Children's Literature for South Africa*, ed. Isabel Cilliers, 198–209. Cape Town: Maskew Miller Longman.

NOTES

1. Amnesty was to be granted to those confessing to crimes associated with a political objective, and occurring between March 1, 1960, and December 5, 1993. Under the rules of the Truth and Reconciliation Commission, indemnity was also granted from prosecution in the courts.

2. For example, a group called the Network of Independent Monitors in South Africa has discovered that White landowners, police, and army members are training militias in the interior of the country. They operate in the guise of legal commando units to protect White farmers who say they are threatened by Blacks, or they are disguised as security companies, or they are trained by pliant tribal chiefs. Intimidation is used to prevent land claims against Whites. (See *The Christian Science Monitor*, August 4, 1998, p. 6.)

PART 1
BACKGROUND

CHAPTER 1

Elements of Apartheid: "Science," Theology, Government, and Extra-Constitutional Government (The Broederbond)

W hen social existence is oppressively regulated, the modern world generally objects. Thus legislators resort to various intellectual strategies to justify anti-democratic policies. They must shape their arguments to correspond with the beliefs of the people who keep them in public office, yet their contentions must accommodate world opinion at some minimal level. Until the post-Nazi era, global opinion was not a great problem in South Africa. Western countries enslaved fifteen million or more Africans between 1451 and 1870, and between 1878 and 1914, European control extended over 84.4 percent of the earth's surface (Pieterse 1992, 52, 76). With this record, the European powers could scarcely take a "holier than thou" attitude toward South Africa. Both at home and abroad "liberalism" sidestepped the ultimate question: equality. This denial of Black/White equality was extensively rationalized in pseudo-scientific studies and rhetoric.

"SCIENCE"

At the heart of scientific racism is the belief in race essentialism, whether this belief surfaces in anthropology, biology, psychology, medicine, or criminology. "Essentialism" in this case means the belief that people have "inherent, unchanging characteristics rooted in biology or in a self-contained culture that explains their status. When linked to oppressions of race, . . . binary thinking ["either/or" thinking] constructs 'essential' group differences" (Collins 1998, 277). Historian Saul Dubow (1989) sees a decline in race essentialism following the terrors it induced in the Nazi years, but ironically it gained momentum in South Africa in the post–World War II years. In 1949, in passing the act that outlawed miscegenation, one government official explained:

> [It is] scientific to hold yourself aloof from a race with a lower civil-isation and less education, and more limited intellectual powers, and of an ethnical type totally different to your own. (quoted in Dubow 1989, 182)

Such ideas had a long history in the "scientific" world, where races were often seen as static creations with permanent cultural and physical elements. Biological inheritances were stressed as the foundation for "natural selection" and the basis for social evolution (ibid, 120). A so-called chain of being with Whites at the advanced end of the chain had been a popular notion since the seventeenth century, and the scientific community in South Africa expanded upon this idea with the publication of *The Bantu-speaking Tribes of South Africa* in 1937. This work was written by thirteen authors, one of which was the anatomist Raymond Dart. He divided Africa into the "Bush," "Brown or Hamitic," and "Negro" races, and his descriptions reveal his "chain" theory with Blacks at the lowest point. He called the Negro skull "infantile in form." The "Bush" skull was "foetal" and the lower jaw retained "primitive features" (Thompson 1995, 100). According to Leonard Thompson, Dart's work had a considerable influence on South African textbooks in the twentieth century.

As late as the 1950s, the skulls of Africans were used as evidence of inferiority. A World Health Organization "expert," Dr. A. Carothers, claimed that the African was equivalent to a European who had experienced a frontal lobotomy (that is, an operation that resulted in psychiatric problems). Thompson reports that the British hired Carothers to supply scientific evidence to use against the Mau Maus, the group challenging British imperial rule in Kenya. Carothers accommodated this political agenda and claimed that Mau Maus were rebelling for their independence because of psychiatric atavism. As a result, the British placed Mau Mau insurgents in special prisons with special "rehabilitation" programs (Thompson 1985, 103–104).

The "science" of eugenics provided practical strategies for preserving a predetermined "racial stock" (i.e., white master race). Eugenics had a tenacious appeal, as seen in 1951 when even the anti-eugenics diplomats who drafted UNESCO documents on brotherhood/sisterhood softened their statements under the influence of geneticists and physical anthropologists—scientists who were trying to sustain their notions about biological determinism.

In the realm of public policy, eugenics supporters even opposed medical services to Blacks. The race purists saw medicine as dysgenic to human advancement when used on behalf of indigenous Africans. Throughout the twentieth century commissions, forums, and societies were created to support theoretical racism and encourage segregationist policies. In a range of lectures and essays, Harold B. Fantham (the first professor of zoology and comparative anatomy at the University of the Wiwatersrand) expressed skepticism about democracy and urged a regulated state based on eugenics principles. To refuse to recognize hereditary difference, he said, would produce "uniform or standardised mediocrity" (quoted in Dubow 1989, 133). While serving as president of the South African Association for the Advancement of Science, Fantham sought to influence policy makers by warning against racial intermixing and the development of a Black urban class (ibid, 135).

This fear of intermixing had an equally vocal group of followers among religionists.

THEOLOGY

The apartheid of Fantham and others in the sciences was echoed with fervent conviction in religious circles. It was God's requirement that the races remain separate and that Whites be in charge of non-Whites. This theological backing for White domination was present in Christian denominations generally, but its existence in the Dutch Reformed Church (*Die Nederduitse Gereformeerde Kerk*) has had the most extensive influence in South African public life.

The story of the Dutch Reformed Church began with the typical missionary efforts in South Africa—that is, the conversion of Africans was the primary agenda. But when Whites moved into African communities to usurp land rights, they refused to hold Communion with Blacks. Thus the Church Synod in 1857 agreed to accommodate this "weakness of some," and conducted segregated church activities. In a document to this effect, the church still maintained that "the Synod considers it . . . according to the Holy Scripture that our heathen members be accepted and initiated into our congregations wherever it is possible" (Ngeokovane 1989, 39). By 1880 the Cape Synod had set up a segregated Mission Church, and soon after the Mission congregations were divided into churches for Africans, Africans of mixed ancestry, and South African Indians. It is significant that these three racial categories were created by the Dutch Reformed Church. Subsequently the same subdivisions remain in place, and their widespread use is understandable, given their early cultural inception.

Before the end of the nineteenth century, references to Holy Scripture changed. Instead of using the Bible as the rationale behind "accepting [heathen members] into our congregation," Holy Scripture was used to justify segregation. For example, Deuteronomy 7 was invoked, a text describing God's orders to the Israelites to avoid mixing with their neighbors (Ngeokovane 1989, 46). In 1898, J. F. Oordt expounded on the Cain/Abel story:

> According to the Boer idea, the Kaffer, the Hottentot, the Bushman belong to a lower race than the Whites. They carry, as a people only rightly called it, the mark of Cain; God, the Lord, destined them to be "drawers of water and hewers of wood," as presses subject to the white race. . . . I do not believe that I go too far when I express my feeling that the Boers as a whole doubt the existence of a Kaffer- or a Hottentot-soul. (quoted in Thompson 1985, 85)

This racist mythology gained in momentum at the close of the Anglo–Boer War in 1902. At that time there were no institutions to embody the newly born Afrikaner solidarity, and the church stepped into this breach. Under these favorable political conditions, the church shifted direction as a public institution and became a significant political movement—one completely intertwined with the policies of the National Party, which was formed in 1914 and came into power in 1924.

In the early twentieth century, Hendrik Frensch Verwoerd (who was minister of "Native" affairs as well as prime minister) explained his belief that Apartheid was an aspect of God's will:

> [T]here is but one way of saving the white races of the world. And that is for the White and non-White in Africa each to exercise his rights within his own areas. . . .
>
> We have been planted here, we believe, with a destiny—destiny not for the sake of the selfishness of a nation, but for the sake of . . . the

service of a nation to the Deity in which it believes . . . (quoted in
Thompson 1985, 69)

Even before the National Party came into power again in 1948,
Church officials met with the then ruling party (the United Party) and
urged its minister of "Native" Affairs to adopt church policies: to prohibit mixed marriages, to prohibit any interracial sexual relations, to
require segregated residential areas, to make school programs for
Africans "suitable for their special character and circumstances" (in
other words, to stick to "servitude education" exclusively). These
policies and others were given concrete legal form between 1949 and
1953 (i.e., in the Prohibition of Mixed Marriages Act, the Immorality
Act, the Group Areas Act, and the "Bantu" Education Act)
(Ngeokovane 1989, 44–45). Of ongoing importance is the policy position related to the franchise. In a booklet in 1951 (*Basic Principles of
Calvinist Christian Political Science*), the church's "Federal Council" stated that "those who have no vote are by no means slaves or oppressed people. . . . Franchise is a treasure, allotted . . . only to those who have
come of age and can use it responsibly before God. Natives do not
meet these requirements. . . ." It is obvious, says this directive, "that
we cannot give the franchise to everyone simply because he is a person" (Ngeokovane 1989, 49).

The Christian Nationalism of South Africa was, according to Saul
Dubow, malleable to some degree in its tendencies and politics, but
fears about racial degeneration remained a constant. A "pure" race
was "to be protected at all costs," and this, according to G. Eloff
(1942) in *Rasse en Rasvermenging* (*Races and Race Mixing*), was "a
holy pledge entrusted to us by our ancestors as part of God's plan with
our People. Any movement, school, or individual who sins against this
must be dealt with as a racial criminal by the effective authorities"
(quoted in Thompson 1995, 184.) In short, God was believed to be
The Great Divider, and mixing could therefore be rightly termed a
morally criminal action. In 1944, S. Du Toit stated in his address "The
Religious Basis of Our Race Policy":

We should not bring together that which God has separated. In pluri-
formity [meaning each group should preserve itself] the counsel of
God is realised. The higher unity lies in Christ and is spiritual in character. Thus there can be no *equalising [gelykstelling]* and no *miscegenation [verbastering]*. (quoted in Dubow 1989, 258–259, emphasis
in original)

We will see these notions alluded to in novels for the young when Blacks are "placed" in certain locations by the expansionist Whites. We will see them in stories that infer a "drawers of water/hewers of wood" role for Blacks. And the "apartness" theory plays a prominent role in anti-miscegenation novels.

The selective use of Christian Scripture to explain Apartheid is a throwback to the slave era, when slavemasters and slavetraders invoked Old Testament stories for their own "moral" defense. It was a purely self-serving tactic in the past, and its appearance in modern South Africa is a similarly self-righteous and self-advancing strategy on the part of the White minority. Historically, given the many groups in the world that have labeled themselves "God's chosen," one wonders how Afrikaners could fail to have at least a few secret doubts on this score.

GOVERNMENT

The underpinnings of Apartheid included official actions that consolidated its structure. These rules and regulations were legislated in increasingly specific terms after the beginning of the twentieth century. This was long before the era known as the Apartheid era—the time following the National Party's 1948 election victory. We will summarize here the way "separateness" was a well-developed policy in the early twentieth century, and then enumerate some of the laws passed after 1948.

In 1912 the organization designed to oppose segregationist policies was founded—the African National Congress—but without Black enfranchisement, this counter force could achieve few reforms. In the industrial sector, White control was extensive enough in 1911 to secure White wages in the gold mining industry at a rate 11.7 times that of Blacks. This advantage did not lessen over time but increased to a rate of 14.7 by 1951.

In the area of land distribution, Blacks were allowed only 7 percent of the land base in 1913, and by 1936 this figure had risen to only 11.7 percent. The Native Land Act of 1913 made it illegal for Africans to own land outside the designated "reserves"—a condition forcing Africans to subsist by working for white farmers. Even sharecropping on White-owned land was made illegal. In essence, the "reserves" were simply a labor pool for White industrialists and farmers (Thompson 1995, 164–165).

The connection between race "separateness" and White financial advantage is revealed in one legislative act after another. In 1922 the Apprenticeship Act devised educational requirements that made Black apprenticeship largely impossible. (Even in 1939, less than 30 percent of African children received any schooling at all, and those in school were at mission schools, usually in the primary grades.) In 1923 the Urban Areas Act gave urban authorities (in partnership with the central government) the power to create African "locations," enforce worker permit requirements, and remove "surplus females" from the "locations" (Thompson 1995, 168–169). In 1924 the Industrial Conciliation Act denied Africans the right to be called "employees"— a move to prohibit Black laborers from negotiating employment rights. When African mine workers called a strike in 1946, twelve Blacks were killed and others were driven back to work at bayonet point. The Chamber of Mines refused to accept any reforms, and pronounced that the "Gold Mining Industry considers that trade-unionism as practiced by Europeans is still beyond the understanding of the Native . . ." (Thompson 1995, 179–180).

By the time the National Party assumed control in 1948, the systematic repression of Africans was commonplace. But Coloured and Asian groups, as well as Africans, came under tighter restrictions after 1948. That was when D. F. Malan (a former minister in the Dutch Reformed Church) became Prime Minister and brought his extremist, "God's chosen" doctrine with him. His reading of Afrikaner history implied a divine *carte blanche* for building a totalitarian system:

> The history of the Afrikaner reveals a determination and a definiteness of purpose which make one feel that Afrikanerdom is not the work of man but a creation of God. We have a Divine right to be Afrikaners. Our history is the highest work of art of the Architect of the centuries. (quoted in Ngeokovane 1989, 54)

Given these convictions, it is not surprising that by 1970 even indirect participation in elections by the "Coloureds" and Asians was abolished. These groups had previously been allowed their own election rolls and the opportunity to vote for a few Whites who would represent their interests in Parliament.

The unique character of the post-1948 era resides in the National Party's reinforcement of pseudo-scientific "biology," plus its theocratically inspired form of tyranny. While segregation was the overriding principle, this "by no means excludes the employment of 'Native' labour for the economic machine of the whites for a long time to come . . . ," as a document from the Dutch Reformed Church made clear (quoted in Ngeokovane 1989, 50). Even a short list of official acts suggests a frantic effort to achieve those twin goals: (1) "separateness" and (2) a supply of human "fuel" for the "economic machine of the whites." For example:

- 1949: Prohibition of Mixed Marriages Act (mixed marriages and interracial sexual relations were forbidden).

- 1950: Population Registration Act (this act established each person's offically sanctioned and mandatory racial category). This meant the dissolution of homes if, for example, one parent was White and one was Coloured.

- 1950: Immorality Act (this tightened the rules of the Prohibition of Mixed Marriages Act).

- 1950: Suppression of Communism Act (communism was broadly defined, and the minister of justice had arbitrary power over anyone suspected of advancing the aims of communism).

- 1950: Group Areas Act (the government divided areas into zones where only designated persons of a specific race could work or live; thus Coloureds and Asians were moved into satellite townships).

- 1953: Reservation of Separate Amenities Act (this act made the unequal conditions of separate public facilities legal).

- 1953: Bantu Education Act (nongovernment schools were closed down, since it was feared that they might teach "alien" ideas; schools for African children were expanded and placed under tight control). (By 1990, this tight control had produced the following pupil/teacher ratios: 16 to 1 in White schools, 50 to 1 in Black schools.)

- 1959: Extension of University Education Act (this act prohibited White colleges from admitting Blacks).

• 1971: Bantu Homelands Constitution Act (this represents a fraud
ulent form of decolonization. "Independence" could be proclaimed
for a "Homeland," and Africans assigned to that area were denied
South African citizenship. The purpose was to keep South Africa
purely White, except for labor purposes. Africans could then come
in on passes as temporary residents. Geographically, the Homelands
were scattered fragments of land and could never develop any real
nationhood) (Thompson 1995, 190–200).

As South Africa approached the 1994 elections, a few of these laws
were rescinded, but the civil service employees who had enforced the
repressive legislation were guaranteed their jobs in the post-Apartheid
period. This highly dubious compromise was made by the ANC to
assuage White fears. The Mandela/DeKlerk negotiators allowed the
Apartheid-era employees to keep their posts until retirement age, and
the most damaging results of this compromise may well be occurring
in the field of education, since South African educationists are heavily
represented in the Afrikaner nationalist organization, the Broederbond
society.

EXTRA-CONSTITUTIONAL GOVERNMENT
(THE BROEDERBOND)

The Broederbond is a secret society that was formed in 1918 to mobi-
lize Afrikaners in their rivalry with the English-speaking South
Africans. Historian J. H. P. Serfontein maintains that "since the early
thirties, [the Broederbond] has played a decisive role in shaping the
history of Afrikaner nationalism" (quoted in Ngeokovane 1989, 59).
Over the years this organization consolidated its power by developing
enterprises that would serve as "fronts"—as distinct entities advancing
its agenda. For example, groups that are, in essence, Broederbond
groups include the Institute for Christian National Education, the
Federation of Afrikaans Cultural Association, and the White Workers'
Protection Society. The latter restricted its membership to White
Protestants and, according to the *Sunday News of Tanzania*, worked
to "propagate a clear determination of which occupations must be
reserved for whites and (blacks)" (Ngeokovane 1989, 60). By 1984, as
reported in the *Financial Mail*:

> Very few senior appointments—whether in the Cabinet, Parliament,
> Provincial Councils, SABC (South African Broadcasting Corporation),

three Afrikaans sister Churches, civil service, defense force, police, sports
bodies, schools, universities and colleges, Afrikaans newspapers, coopera-
tives, control boards or parastatals—went to non-broeders. (quoted in
Ngeokovane 1989, 61)

To say that such influence represents an extra-constitutional government is not, in our view, an overstatement. All prime ministers during the Apartheid era and prior to DeKlerk were members of the
Broederbond. In the government of DeKlerk's immediate predecessor,
P. W. Botha, all the Cabinet members except two were also "Bond"
members.

So what is Broederbond philosophy? Six of its tenets were publicized in an Afrikaner newspaper in 1944 and 1945: full international
independence, an end to the inferiority of the Afrikaans language in
the organization of the State, the separation of all "non-white races"
and their guardianship under Whites, assurance of work for all White
citizens, nationalization of the money market and systematic coordi-
nation of economic policies, and the Afrikanerization of education in
a Christian National spirit (Ngeokovane 1989, 63–64). Since these
principles were often clandestinely implemented, Parliament issued
occasional calls for the investigation of the Broederbond. But the
investigators were Cabinet ministers who belonged either to the
Broederbond or the Dutch Reformed Church, and predictably they
found the organization to be "healthy"—even a promoter of "good
relations" between the English- and Afrikaans-speaking peoples.

Cecil Ngeokovane, who is both a clergyman and historian, sums up
his conclusions after an extensive study of the Broederbond's historical and ongoing role. He writes: "There is no doubt that it is the
Broederbond that governs South Africa" (1989, 72).

****

Apartheid can be understood as a set of highly integrated elements.
With reference to scientific racism, Saul Dubow (1989) notes that "it
is possible to locate the science of race as 'part of the project of nationalism'" (286). Leonard Thompson (1985) calls one of his books *The
Political Mythology of Apartheid*; a mythology is woven with many
strands. In the White South African community (especially the
Afrikaner group), the strands consist of ideas about divine intervention, biological inevitability, and historical events.

These ideas had strong social and professional institutions to teach and disseminate their main tenets, including eugenics, which combined pseudo-science and public policy. They incorporated the Dutch Reformed Church and its articulation of the "God's Chosen People" myth. To give history a Christian Nationalist spin, patriotic organizations such as the Broederbond devised their own interpretations of Black/White and English/Dutch historical evolution.

Given the totalitarian nature of Apartheid, it follows that an Apartheid-controlled educational system will circulate widely the white supremacist mythology. Thus children have learned the rightness of White "science," theology, and government, while Black history has been largely distorted or concealed. Generally speaking, the Black Consciouness Movement and the steadily evolving resistance movements have not appeared in South African children's novels except in ways that discredit them. Moreover, one of the heroic stories of the twentieth century concerns the role of Black children in the democratic movement, yet children's literature does not truthfully represent this story. Perhaps this omission is not so surprising, since the "gatekeepers" of literary education have been part of the same totalitarian system as the bureaucrats.

WORKS CITED

Collins, Patricia Hill. 1998. *Fighting Words: Black Women and the Search for Justice.* Minneapolis and London: University of Minnesota Press.

Dubow, Saul. 1989. *Scientific Racism in Modern South Africa.* Cambridge: Cambridge University Press.

Eloff, Gerhardus. 1992. *Rasse en Rasvermenging* (Races and Race Mixing). Bloemfontein: Nationale pers bpk.

Ngeokovane, Cecil. 1989. *Demons of Apartheid: A Moral and Ethical Analysis of the N.G.K., N.P. and Broederbond's Justification of Apartheid.* Braamfontein, S.A.: Skotaville Publishers (Incorporated Association not for Gain).

Pieterse, Jan Nederveen. 1942. *White on Black: Images of Africa and Blacks in Western Popular Culture.* New Haven and London: Yale University Press.

Thompson, Leonard. 1995. *A History of South Africa.* Rev. ed. New Haven and London: Yale University Press.

Thompson, Leonard. 1985. *The Political Mythology of Apartheid.* New Haven and London: Yale University Press.

CHAPTER 2

"Gatekeepers" and Literary Education

I n discussing a "New South Africa," book specialists have been grappling with several questions: Who should write South African literature about Blacks? Who should critique it and take charge of its circulation? Such a discussion about the "new" is inevitably linked with concerns about the "old." On the one hand, Black South Africans and writers in exile do not usually downplay the horrors of Apartheid. They recognize that historical accuracy in education means first overturning Apartheid's educational structure—the race-biased curriculums and teaching materials that send white supremacist messages. For these anti-Apartheid artists and educators, the colonizer can no longer be allowed to exercise intellectual authority over the colonized.

On the other hand, White South African book specialists (as well as some in Britain and America) suggest either a gradualist approach to educational reform or an amnesia-like silence. This strategy amounts to a feigned innocence about decades of miseducation. It amounts to what Patricia J. Williams (1997) calls "the transgressive refusal to know" in her comment about a similar "color-blindness" in the United States of America and the United Kingdom (27).

An example of this "transgressive refusal" occurs in Anthony Adams's observations in *Reading Against Racism* (1992), an anthology from Britain's Open University Press. Adams rejects an anti-racist educational movement, although he concedes that within newly conceived pluralist societies "there is still a great deal of prejudice and intolerance of which education . . . must take account" (xii). He writes:

A possible problem with this is, however, the feeling that by its very nature "anti-racist" education has to be somewhat negative, making people feel guilty for the racism of their own attitudes and those of people around them. This was certainly true of much of the original movement towards anti-racist education in schools, a good deal of which had a strongly felt political ideology at its heart. While many of us might share this ideology, it remains the case that a more positive approach to the issue would be welcome and move it away from the danger of sloganizing and propaganda, even in the best of causes. (xii)

This statement supports the status quo. It urges people to reject guilt about the past; it suggests that a liberationist ideology be muffled because it is "political" (as if facist ideologies are *not* political); it categorizes anti-racism as "negative" (as if opposing injustice *could* be negative); it calls anti-racist education "propaganda" (as if pro-racist education is mysteriously devoid of propaganda); it pleads for a "more positive approach" (as if equality, democracy, justice, and anti-colonialism can be *less* than positive). In a word, what Adams is doing is painting liberationists as extremists, while showing the anti-democracy group as benignly moderate and rational. This is a familiar conservative ploy.

Anthony Adams is a lecturer in education at the University of Cambridge and the general editor of the Open University Press's series "English, Language, and Education." The editor for the specific South African essay in *Reading Against Racism* is Emrys Evans, and in his introduction he echoes Adams's cautionary stance:

There has been some evidence in recent years that the hasty deployment of deliberate anti-racist or multiracial programmes in schools is not always effective, and can even prove counterproductive, underlining differences without establishing how difference itself can be rewarding. (1992, 7)

Have anti-racist programs ever existed without being "deliberate"? Is "hasty deployment" a danger here, given the way anti-racist education has already been delayed until the end of the century and is still an uphill battle?

Evans is concerned about censorship and argues that a literature teacher does "not need to protect [his/her] students from even the most overtly racist material . . ." (6). As an example of racism he cites the "cheap" and "nasty" African kings in Dickens's *Our Mutual Friend*. He says he did not even notice these offensive characterizations until a second reading (a point that says more about him than about how children should be educated). Arguing against "protection" of students, he does not weigh the consequences in terms of either cultural domination or free speech. A. Sivanandan (1995), editor of *Race and Class*, sees self-serving appeals to free speech as a conservative tactic. He comments:

> Anybody who uses the freedom of speech to deny others their basic freedoms is not a democrat but a totalitarian. Freedom of speech in such hands is no longer a principle but a tactic, and when it is debased to that level, it is no longer freedom of speech as we know it. (79)

A basic freedom that supercedes freedom of speech, says Sivanandan, is the freedom of life.

The specific South African essay in Evans's (1992) anthology is by Denise Newfield, a lecturer in English education at the University of the Witwatersrand. She trains secondary school teachers, and is described by Evans as one who "has been concerned to modify the curriculum . . . in order to make it appropriate and relevant to all South Africans" (ix). But can Newfield's approach fulfill this goal? She urges a new curriculum (one that is "oppositional" vis-à-vis racist texts), but her method seems largely ineffectual. In her "oppositional" teaching mode, students are "to discuss the racist and imperialist prejudices [texts] contain" (as for example in *King Solomon's Mines* [1885]). They are to "put them into historical perspective" and "reveal whose interests are served" (44). But even if South Africa had a teachers' corps to carry out this mandate, assigning a novel such as *King Solomon's Mines* could hardly produce an "oppositional" experience for the youngsters. Haggard's novel is a potboiler—a spellbinding melodrama that has mesmerized young and old for more than a century. Its popularity is so unshakeable that Hollywood filmmakers have re-made it four times. Its cultural prejudices (not to mention its sensationalism) can scarcely be countered by the anti-Apartheid literature Newfield mentions (i.e., William Plomer's *Turbott Wolfe* and Es'kia Mphahlele's *Down Second Avenue*). Moreover, Newfield's own reading of Haggard's novel seems decidedly less than "oppositional." She writes:

> Although Allan Quatermain, Haggard's narrator, is sympathetic to the "natives," and not overtly racist, in the end his views are segregationist, as we see in the outcome of the love affair between Foulata and Captain Good, one of the three English travellers. (1992, 44)

Newfield misreads when she fails to perceive the novel's ubiquitous, overt racism. This is the most serious drawback in an essay that in many ways pleads the anti-Apartheid cause.

Another strategic way to oppose Apartheid is through the use of texts in indigenous languages. Newfield points to those prepared by the South African "Storyteller Group," texts targeting primarily the "disadvantaged black readers" living a "South African township culture" (57). But as the Storytelling Group creates literature for a post-apartheid society, it also downplays the recent past. The Group wants, it says, a literature that helps township children overcome resentment:

> To break free of the apartheid chrysalis we need, above all, to boldly project images of "what can be." We need to "*pull*" people with a vision of the future, not "*push*" them with the guilt and resentment of the past. (Napper and Esterhuysen, 1990, 14)

The idea that guilt must not intrude upon the healing process in the "new" South Africa can be a misguided notion. It depends upon whose guilt and whose culpability.

Poet Dennis Brutus (1994) comments about a continuing challenge rather than an imagined transformation. He points to the necessity of marshalling resources before a material change can be realized: "I don't think it helps to be optimistic if there is no money in the bank. It's really not going to save you" (109). He adds:

> I find it quite intriguing that People who are on the Left should be saying, "Let's hear less about the struggle." And I'm not altogether comfortable with it; it seems to me not consistent. For one thing I don't think you can dismiss the past. . . . I can sympathize with the notion that you don't want a preoccupation with persecution and oppression . . . [but] I think that's unsound [i.e., calling protest literature not valid now], because . . . it's a mistake to turn your back on it, and I think if you cut off your own stream of the tradition, you are not going to benefit by it, having to start all over again. (109)

Brutus's insights about the need for historical and cultural honesty are applicable to both writers and critics of children's books.

Another issue that concerns "gatekeepers" is the possibility that works for the young may be "political." They see such a theme as a drag on South Africa's renewal. In *Crossing Over: Stories for a New South Africa* (1995), Jakes Gerwel mentions the need for "crossing . . . a divide which [goes] beyond the obviously political: . . . a loosening of the paralysing bonds of fear and suspicion, . . . the possibility of . . . speaking about pain without unleashing destruction, the emancipation of the personal from the overbearing domination of the political" (unpaged). Gerwel notes that South African society "has made a remarkable transition," and given that metamorphosis, political themes have become obsolete. This euphoria is not shared by those in the actual political sphere. Political scientist Margaret Carol Lee (1995) emphasizes the ongoing struggle to achieve real reforms. She highlights the conflict "between those who support the further consolidation of democracy and those who seemingly oppose it" (2). Similarly Nelson Mandela (1997) (three years after his election) notes the entrenched nature of anti-democratic forces:

> Because we have just begun, the process of fundamental social transformation has not yet impacted seriously on the apartheid paradigm which affects all aspects of our lives. . . . This process has therefore not yet tested the strength of the counter-offensive which would seek to maintain the privileges of the white minority. . . . The desire to maintain these privileges has been demonstrated consistently during the [recent] period . . . (2–3)

Maintaining White minority privilege relates directly to current issues in children's literature. For example, why are White South Africans "standing in" for Blacks and attempting to invent the Black voice? In the essay "Who Can Tell My Story?" African American novelist Jacqueline Woodson (1998) addresses the same concern in an American context. She describes her encounter with a White author writing about Blacks: "What people of color do you know?" asked Woodson. "Well," replied the White author, "it's based on a family that used to work for mine" (38). Woodson comments:

> This family had stepped inside this woman's kitchen, but she had not been inside theirs. And having not sat down to their table, how could

she possibly know the language and the experiences and the feelings there? . . . My belief is that there is room in the world for all stories, and that everyone has one. My hope is that those who write about the tears and the laughter and the language in my grandmother's house have first sat down at the table with us and dipped the bread of their own experiences into our stew. (38)

As Woodson's concerns rest on the foundation of American segregation, so Black South Africans question the veracity of some books on similar grounds. The published children's authors in South Africa are overwhelmingly White, and when they write about Blacks they either see them as servants or as violent township extremists who are challenging their status. As Woodson would say, the "masters" of South Africa have not sat at the table; they have been *served* at table by a powerless, colonized work force.

When book critics ask for an "emancipation . . . from the overbearing domination of the political" (Gerwel 1995, unpaged) they are ignoring or evading an ongoing political contest. In fact the language itself is "a vehicle for the enunciation of political aspirations" (Parker 1978, 3). Referring to the corrupted language of Apartheid as "doublespeak," Kenneth Parker lists the following examples: "political protest is a 'riot,' humans are 'located' and the maintenance of the system is justified as the 'restoration of law and order'" (1–2). In just this way colonialist discourse debases the very stock in trade of the writer: the language itself. So how "do we assess literature in the context of a society . . . where words and their meanings (so crucial for a writer) are invariably corrupted?" (Parker 1978, 2). Even in the law, words become absurd, as Parker demonstrates:

- The Citizenship Act does not confer citizenship but withholds it.
- The Extension of University Education Act prohibits Blacks from attending so-called open universities.
- The Industrial Conciliation Act *divides* labor unions along racial lines and favors Whites in the job market.
- The Publications and Entertainments Act stifles artistic creativity through a strict system of censorship (2).

All of these acts are aimed at the subjugation of indigenous Africans, and the very vocabulary has been distorted for political ends. In contrast, a pro-African vocabulary is largely missing in the ever-present state-run institutions.

Children's book institutions exacerbate the "doublespeak" by proclaiming a "new age"—an allegedly apolitical world—that the narratives themselves do not reflect.

WORKS CITED

Adams, Anthony. 1992. General Editor's Introduction. In *Reading Against Racism*, ed. Emrys Evans, xi–xiii. Buckingham, UK, and Philadelphia, USA: Open University Press.

Brutus, Dennis. 1994. "On a Knife Edge." *Matatu* 11: 101–110.

Evans, Emrys. 1992. Introduction. In *Reading Against Racism*, ed. Emrys Evans, 1–8. Buckingham, UK, and Philadephia, USA: Open University Press.

Gerwel, Jakes. 1995. "Foreword." In *Crossing Over: Stories for a New South Africa*, eds. Linda Rode and Jakes Gerwel, unpaged. Cape Town: Kwela Books.

Lee, Margaret Carol. 1995. "Focus on South Africa: Prospects for the 21st Century." *The Africanist* 3: 2–8, 18.

Mandela, Nelson. 1997. "Report by the President of the ANC, Nelson Mandela," 2–3. Presented at the 50th National Conference of the ANC.

Napper, N. and P. Esterhuysen. 1990. *Popular Literature*. Johannesburg: The Storyteller Group.

Newfield, Denise. 1992. "Reading Against Racism in South Africa." In *Reading Against Racism*, ed. Emrys Evans, 38–63. Buckingham, UK, and Philadelphia, USA: Open University Press.

Parker, Kenneth, ed. 1978. "The South African Novel in English." In *The South African Novel in English: Essays in Criticism and Society*, ed. Kenneth Parker, 1–26. New York: Africana Publishing Co.

Sivanandan, A. 1995. "Fighting Our Fundamentalisms: An Interview with A. Sivanandan." *Race and Class* 36: 3.

Williams, Patricia J. 1997. *Seeing a Color-Blind Future: The Paradox of Race.* New York: Noonday Press (Farrar, Straus, & Giroux).

Woodson, Jacqueline. 1998. "Who Can Tell My Story?" *Horn Book* Jan/Feb: 34–38.

PART 2

NOVELS ABOUT CONTEMPORARY SOUTH AFRICA

CHAPTER 3

Civil Disobedience and Urban Conflict: The Apartheid Perspective

S outh Africa's urban strife has been about civil and human rights for Blacks, "Coloreds," and Asians. Behind this issue is the all-important issue of labor rights. Apartheid, like its colonialist framework, is about the theft of African wealth, including the appropriation of African labor. The novels we discuss in this chapter not only obfuscate this issue but also depict people of color as incapable of positive action and therefore a hindrance to democratic reforms. These representations make Africans look as if they *belong* in the subservient labor pool to which Apartheid assigns them.

Maretha Maartens's *The Ink Bird* (1989) (retitled in the West as *The Paper Bird*), Barbara Ludman's *The Day of the Kugel* (1989), and Elana Bregin's *The Slayer of Shadows* (1995) present a blatant reversal of heroes and wrongdoers in recent South African urban history. In *The Ink Bird*, labor unions and their child supporters are cast in the villain's role, while the police are not a real threat despite their noisy trucks and helicopters. In *The Day of the Kugel*, White college students battle the police, and in the end these anti-government protesters are set up as noble, self-sacrificing role models. The Black protagonist becomes a turncoat, a traitor to the anti-Apartheid movement. *The Ink Bird* features a largely Black cast of characters, while *The Day of the Kugel* concentrates on Whites, but in both novels the European South Africans are the agents of benevolence and come across as the best hope of South Africa. The implication is that Whites exclusively "own" South Africa and should continue to do so. The same holds true for Bregin's *The Slayer of Shadows*. This novel dwells so obsessively on alleged Black sadism that the colonialist, pre-election message is strongly reinforced—namely, the necessity of White rule. As the hero says about life in post-Apartheid South Africa: "We are less free than we ever were" (7).

THE INK BIRD (RETITLED: THE PAPER BIRD)

The coalition between Black students and industrial workers was one of the most fruitful and constructive developments in the anti-Apartheid movement, and this is the history that Maretha Maartens turns upside down in *The Ink Bird*.[1] From her perspective, student boycotts that were in alignment with worker "stay-aways" had no redeeming elements. Instead the politically active students are mere criminals—the instigators of unspeakable tortures, murders, and intimidations. This is the pro-Apartheid propaganda line. As demands increased in the 1980s for Nelson Mandela's release from a twenty-seven year imprisonment, children's book writers often discredited Black political action. For decades student strikes had been carrying some of the burden that worker strikes could not carry. School children could boycott the Establishment indefinitely, whereas wage-earners (who had families to feed) could not. Moreover, school "stay-aways" caught the attention and sympathy of the international community. The young dissidents were able to undermine the government's major propaganda point—namely, that Apartheid was being reformed along democratic lines. Black child martyrs shattered the spurious claim that South Africa belonged to the "Christian democratic West."

Civil disobedience as we understand it is a way of demonstrating dissatisfaction. The children of Soweto and elsewhere were within their legal rights to express their disapproval on matters affecting their education, their life, and their future. Most of these children witnessed the torture and dehumanization inflicted on their parents and grandparents. They knew that they were next in line for the slow annihilation being implemented by the Apartheid government. In *The Ink Bird* Maartens offers little if any insight into why the Black children chose to abandon school and directly challenge Apartheid's ruthless security forces.

The central plot line revolves around Adam, a young newsboy who opposes a work stoppage since his mother depends upon his wages. Actually the call for a "stay-away" is *about* wages—about overturning the system that keeps Adam's family on the brink of starvation and ill health. Adam's deceased father had taught his children the importance of prayer, but Adam feels abandoned by God when student protesters threaten to burn the houses of all those failing to comply with the work stoppage. (Predictably, a White man helps Adam survive, and the boy concludes that "not everybody wants to kill and burn" [89]). Maartens turns all the democratic activists into killers and burners, as well as people who deny God. The use of religion to prop up Apartheid has historical resonance. Adam hears essentially the same sermon that was preached to slaves: If you pray you will know that God is with you despite your misery. The child's White benefactor says:

> "We're all scared, Adam . . . I'm scared too . . . of the long nights . . .
> of getting old and dying. We're all scared. But we're not alone, Adam.
> The Lord is still there. . . . He hasn't forgotten us, Adam. . . .
> Tomorrow you'll get up and know that He was here when you were
> afraid. (79)

The speaker here is Old Hansie, an elderly White man who also makes his living selling newspapers. Maartens builds much of her argument around the idea that everyone has problems, everyone is scared. She places Old Hansie within the lower classes despite his "superior" race. A White newsboy is abused by his alcoholic family, and this supposedly proves that problems simply come in different forms to different groups. Apparently Adam and the readers of this book are to believe that the anti-Apartheid demonstrators have no legitimate cause for their rebellion. They should do as the White characters and not whine about their problems. This is a smokescreen to hide the scope and severity of government-based oppressions against Blacks. Wherever Maartens reveals severe conditions in Black townships, she simultaneously shifts the burden of responsibility to the township inhabitants. For example, she surrounds Adam and his family with grotesquely mean-spirited relatives; Adam's cousins are critical and abusive. Virtually all African characters are delineated in pointlessly negative terms: "Mama Dora [Adam's aunt] had legs like tree trunks . . ."(3). Adam's mother (being pregnant) is compared to a cow that has swallowed a plastic bag (5). The characters wander aimlessly as if in a daze, unable to respond intelligently to the cruel realities of township life. This approach to character obscures the actual cause and effect relationships that the reading audience should understand about township chaos. If the truth were told, we would see that health problems, school shortages, and labor strikes *can* be largely explained by official decrees—by policies that denied fair wages, adequate hospital access, and sufficient school facilities to Blacks.

The Real and Imagined Health Conditions

Health problems are so pervasive in *The Ink Bird* that we could follow the plot line by moving from one to another: from malnutrition, to a baby's diseased ear, to the mistreatment of newborns, to an incapacitating case of influenza. They have the potential of bringing to the reader either a realistic or distorted picture of township health issues, but Maartens provides the latter. She places the fault of poor health on township residents rather than official policies. This is not a minor oversight, since the denial of health care for Blacks is one of Apartheid's most glaring denials of human rights.

When Adam's mother travels by taxi to a hospital, gives birth to twins, and immediately returns home in another taxi, why is her hospitalization so inexplicably brief? Is there no space for herself and the babies? Is there no way to pay the doctors? Is she happier at home where there is practically no food for any of her children? Should we even wonder about these harmful conditions since a life of bare survival is to be considered the norm for Blacks? If any truthful cause and effect relationships were established in these episodes, we would be given some idea as to why the health facilities are so sparse—why the hero's anxieties often revolve around the ill health in his family. We would not be asked to view such harsh circumstances as "just the way it is."

The conditions Adam's family would really encounter can be at least estimated by statistics collected for Soweto—a township with facilities at Baragwanath Hospital. This institution allegedly offers "superior medical care . . . compared to their counterparts elsewhere in Africa," but in winter, according to Dr. Aziza Seedat (1987), "bed occupancy in the medical and surgical wards can be up to 300 percent and 250 percent respectively" (173). He notes that when members of the press visited the hospital in 1976 they found that "the situation at Baragwanath was one patient under the bed, two in the bed and two on the floor" (173). In her novel Maartens describes Adam's mother's brief hospitalization during the delivery of her twins, but this, in reality, would probably not have been her choice. Dr. Seedat reports: "Because of the critical shortage of beds, over 13,000 patients are discharged each year before their treatment is complete . . ."(174).

Because there are not enough doctors, a red sticker marked "Urgent" is stuck to the forehead of those patients who are the most critically ill. Some patients are moved outside during the day to allow doctors more space inside. Medical records are often lost, even those reporting what medication a patient is receiving. Dirty blankets are unwashed before being reused (174).

In maternity units in Port Elizabeth and in Atteridgeville, Pretoria, women in labor were lying two to a bed or lying on the floor and on hospital trolleys. Alongside these wards were the White sections of the hospital containing empty beds (174).

One of the most harmful hospital regulations had to do with the exclusion of one group from a hospital reserved for another. Young children, as well as adults, often died because they were turned away or because an ambulance would not serve them. No matter how serious the injury, racial segregation was absolute, and easily correctible illnesses became lethal illnesses when denied treatment (Seedat 1987, 175). In *The Ink Bird*, Adam's youngest sister cries pitifully throughout the whole novel because of an excruciating earache, a problem that could have undoubtedly been relieved at least to some degree.

Besides relating health issues to newborns, Maartens introduces child health care when Adam comes down with the flu. His care is dependent on Whites, as when Adam is discovered in the city, sleeping under some stairs. He is already having serious symptoms, but the White man who finds him does not call the police. This is to be viewed by readers, apparently, as a beneficent act. The man leaves him alone in the freezing weather, under an outdoor staircase. He feels no obligation to find adequate shelter for the boy; he supplies no blankets, coats, food, or medicine. His kindness reaches no further than a refusal to press charges and have the boy locked up. In the end, Old Hansie offers Adam his bed and the medicine he uses on himself, and Adam immediately recovers.

With an equal lack of credibility, the novelist describes malnutrition, the "single biggest killer of black children in South Africa" (Seedat 1987, 171). Government propaganda treats this tragedy as self-imposed, insisting that Blacks are too ignorant to feed their children well, or too mesmerized by superstition and eating taboos (171). In 1980, the staff at a Bophuthatswana Hospital (an institution serving 100,000 people) claimed that as "many as 40 percent of deaths were due to malnutrition" (172). In 1983 it was reported by the head of pediatrics at the University of Natal that the malnutrition death toll was three to four per hour! The majority of these victims were children (172). When Dr. Seedat complained to the government, he was told that Blacks should stop the tendency to "multiply uncontrollably" (172). This is a common retort, a way to shift responsibility to the sufferers.

The Student/Laborer Coalition

In relation to schooling, Maartens portrays the school boycott as an opportunity to play hooky, as well as an opportunity to commit sadistic acts. This ignores the boycott's ties to labor-directed work stoppages. By the time Maartens created this novel in 1989, laborer/student solidarity had been operating for at least two decades, and it had succeeded in rallying much of the world to the anti-Apartheid cause. It had spurred the establishment of economic boycotts against South Africa in much of the industrialized world. Instead of being truants and murderous thugs, the students were helping the world discover its social conscience.

However, it must be admitted that revolutionary conditions often open the door to those people who want to capitalize upon the turbulence and use it for personal gain. In short, criminal incursions into any liberation movement do occur. The "Tsotsis" (the young delinquents) in South Africa were, however, victims more than perpetrators of crime—victims of state-produced hardships, injustices, and gross violations of human rights. According to Jeremy Seekings (1993) in his study of youth politics in the 1980s, the Tsotsis were an offshoot of poverty, lack of opportunity, and lack of responsible channels for activity. They were acclimatized to fighting when no alternative lifestyle was available. The realities of their lives typically included a three-year waiting period before finding a job when schooling ended. It included shifting "from job to job, retrenchment to retrenchment," as well as a lack of necessary qualifications in an increasingly high tech society (Seekings 1993, 14). Moreover, the uprootedness caused by the forced removal of whole communities sparked an increase in gang activity (14).

Despite forced removals and other hardships, community initiatives to build schools were not allowed to succeed. African-owned private schools were shut down by the government. For example, the Lwandle school was a private facility established in 1987 by fathers who lived in a hostel. The numerous state schools in their area did not admit Africans, and the children had no school at all unless they commuted to a school twenty-five kilometers away (Jones 1993, 165). In trying to obtain an unused hall for use as a preschool, the parents were told that "the children did not exist officially" (166).

Despite so many barriers, the young people shaped themselves into a largely constructive and progressive force that could sustain a boycott over time. This was important because those in the working-class had fewer available tactics for the long-term battle. Still, independent labor unions emerged as a significant force in the 1980s. In 1985 they joined together as a "super-federation"—the Congress of South African Trade Unions (COSATU) (Callinicos 1988, 59–60). The termination of labor recruiting opportunities in such countries as Malawi and Mozambique worked in labor's favor (i.e., Malawi banned recruitment of its citizens for South African mines, and fewer workers could be hired in Mozambique when FRELIMO, the Mozambique liberation movement, met with success) (26). Even while the "Bantu education" policies sparked the 1976 student rebellion in Soweto, it was an overall shifting of power between White capital and Black labor that underlay the student uprising (26).

One education policy that students rejected was the requirement that half of all secondary school subjects be taught exclusively in Afrikaans. Student resistance peaked on June 16, 1976, and spread geographically throughout regions of the country and from schools to factories. On the worker side, three massive strikes were called in 1976. On the student side, the young rebels persisted until the Soweto Urban Bantu Council was forced to resign the following year. According to historian Alex Callinicos (1988), this Council was one of the Apartheid government's many "stooges" (27).

What Maartens fails to show is that children were such a vitally important part of this process of political change. Instead, her plot line blames the strikes on youthful criminals or on children being manipulated politically—a view that serves as an apology for state repression. Youthful participants are portrayed as destructive and self-serving, but what transpired could hardly be called the result of self-interest: there were seven hundred recorded deaths, there were mass detentions, there was a thorough suppression of the Black Consciousness Movement. Moreover, the only course for thousands of Black youngsters was to escape into exile (Callinicos 1988, 27).

A Frequent Apartheid Ally: Religion

God is introduced early to show how young Adam is divinely led to adopt the government's perspective—namely, that the Black quest for labor rights was a completely ignoble movement.

Maartens leans upon Biblical authority in various ways that suggest Western rather than African thought. For example, she presents the African God ("Modimo") as a source of intellectual confusion. When the Casspir guns and police commands are terrifying Adam's sister, we are told that "Adam, in fear, tried to pray, but he became completely confused. The great voice outside now sounded like Modimo's. In reflection, Adam thought: Was he in heaven? . . . or in the Casspirs . . . ?" (7). This kind of disbelief is not typically African. In Adam's belief system, Modimo is the creator almighty, and African children are brought up to believe in the Creator (God/Modimo) without questioning Modimo's supernatural power and authority. There was no Martin Luther in Africa who broke away from the Catholic church to create his own faith. There was no "*divine* right of kings" as proclaimed by Henry VIII. But Maartens finds the Old Testament useful as a method of forewarning Adam about the supposedly immoral labor and school protests—about how the work stoppages stem from intimidation from revolutionaries. She introduces the story of Sodom and Gomorrah. Sodom, with all its negative connotations, is what Adam sees when his community is launching political demonstrations. When Adam violates the work stoppage and walks to work, we see his state of mind:

> [Adam] felt like Lot when Sodom and Gomorrah were burning behind him. You're done for if you look back, Lot, the angel had said. One glance and you'll be turned into a pillar of salt. (55)

Adam kept this warning in mind until he stumbled over the bicycle wheel he was using as a toy. Then he peered between his legs and behind him was "an upside-down world." "So Sodom and Gomorrah must have seemed to Lot and his wife" (55). In the Biblical tale, God did listen to Abraham's pleas when Abraham bargained with Him to save the two cities, but no negotiations were underway between the Apartheid government and the Black protesters. Maartens takes only the government side, contriving Old Hansie as the teacher who would instruct Adam about "hope" and "goodness."

Whether introducing the subjects of health, schooling, or religion,

Maartens creates a great information vacuum in *The Ink Bird*. The presence of some political content in the book does not mean that the novel is politically neutral or politically noncommittal. Reviewer Carolyn Phelan (1991) writes that readers will "learn little about [South Africa's] politics, social strata, or factional violence," but in this comment she is overlooking the politics of an anti-Black authorial slant (137). She speaks approvingly of the novel as "sensitive" and "unsentimental"—as a universal treatment of "what it means to be poor, hungry, and terrified" (137). This claim about the "sensitive" and "universal" points to Phelan's political position, just as Maartens's story points to an Apartheid-based rationale.

Another commentator, Jay Heale (1996), is on even shakier ground. He applauds Maartens for "creating an understanding across cultural and colour barriers" (23). He writes that *The Ink Bird* has "[opened] blinkered eyes to the life lived by people whom most South African children were unlikely to meet" (37). Actually, "most South African children" *are those Black children* Maartens misrepresents. How can Heale refer to "most South African children" when he means only the small fraction of White children? His inference that South Africa is essentially a White nation is the fallacy that lies behind the whole Apartheid program.

THE DAY OF THE KUGEL

Barbara Ludman's novel is essentially a story about *noblesse oblige*.[2] Whites of high rank do noble deeds at the time of the 1976 Soweto uprisings. The protagonist, sixteen-year-old Michelle, compares this moment with 1966 and the Selma march led by Martin Luther King, Jr. As a White American child, she had heard reports of that event in her early years. As the novel opens, she is arriving in Johannesburg in 1976 to live with an aunt who is married to a politically active White law professor.

It is hard to ignore a comparison between Ludman's novel and the *noblesse oblige* fiction produced by White antebellum abolitionists in the United States. As in the free-the-slaves narratives, White intellectuals go out of their way to support Black liberation. They tutor Black children, they smuggle arms and people across borders, they give legal advice, they pay college fees, they join marches. In these self-congratulatory tales they depict Blacks as eternally grateful: as contented with their subservient positions, as awestruck by White courage, as impressed by White wisdom, as amazed by the Caucasian's talent for bonding with little Black children.

At the same time, both abolitionist and Apartheid-related authors carefully lend credence to conventional stereotypes about Blacks. They accentuate the idea of potential good will and good relations, but they also imply that Blacks are not ready for full participation in the civic community.

These reservations are introduced into *The Day of the Kugel* in various ways. In some episodes, Black and White experiences are paired so as to highlight the unreadiness of the Black characters for full liberation. For example, Clive (Michelle's teenage cousin) is a modern Scarlet Pimpernel: a Revolutionary masquerading as a conceited, upper-crust cad. In the end we learn that he has been risking life and limb to aid the anti-Apartheid movement (smuggling guns, etc.). His revolutionary counterpart is Joe, a Black waiter at an Afrikaner-owned restaurant near Witwatersrand University. He is a banned playwright, and Michelle's lawyer-uncle has managed to have his sentence "relaxed."

Ludman draws a contrast between these two young men by depicting a heroic Clive and a traitorous Joe. Joe is arrested for circulating an illegal handbill, and he "turns state's evidence" in return for a light sentence (four to five years in prison). The incriminating evidence includes tattling on Stephen, the printer of the handbill. Joe is now sharply contrasted with Stephen, a paragon of unselfed service, a tireless tutor of poorly educated Blacks. As Stephen flees from the police, Michelle (his girlfriend) steps into his tutoring role. She has changed from a rebellious, bad-tempered brat (whose movie star parents will not raise her) to a responsible revolutionary insurgent.

Another pairing is between Michelle and Beauty. Michelle's aunt has found her niece a job at the restaurant where Joe and Beauty work. The latter is described as either too lazy or too incompetent to do even the simplest kitchen tasks. She is so slow that her employer despairs of ever having enough potatoes for her customers. Michelle has the same assignment and although she is clumsy as a potato peeler, she learns fast. Beauty plays no role in the narrative except as a means of illustrating Michelle's dexterity and overall intelligence in contrast to Beauty's mental and physical backwardness.

Other Black characters include Alice (the aunt's housekeeper), her daughter (a teacher in one of the closed-down schools), and her grandson, Sipho. Alice has only one half-day off per week and lives in what is virtually a cell (a space the size of a typical bathroom). Yet she is full of gratitude, good-humor, and deep devotion for Michelle when this teenager turns protester.

As the main protagonist, Michelle is revealing more than what the author may have intended, since some readers will notice the disparity between what this rich White girl suffers and the suffering of Blacks. The novel's book jacket describes the teenager's trauma: "Michelle has been passed down from relative to relative. . . . Now she's in a new country, South Africa, and she is surrounded by things that she doesn't understand." This kind of trauma is miniscule in contrast to what is actually experienced by indigenous Africans in that era. Political commentator Conor Cruise O'Brien (1987) writes:

> [Black Africans] having once been South Africans, suddeny found themselves citizens of Transkei. Then they were out of Transkei and back into South Africa, because the boss of Transkei, Kaizer Matanzima, didn't like them. Then they were out of South Africa again and found themselves citizens of the newly created and now "Independent" state of Ciskei . . . (455)

If Michelle sometimes woke up and "could not immediately recall where she was. Washington? Atlanta?" (1) then how did Africans feel when packed like cattle in trucks and driven to a no man's land? They had no jobs, no provisions, no security; they were often separated from friends and family and wrenched from their loved ones repeatedly.

Michelle is given that casualness that defines a way of life, that presents an attitude that is relatively free from tension, frustration, and the complexities of difference. Yet Ludman wants to take Michelle out of the "Kugel" category (a Kugel being a "disgusting, dull, boring noodle puddling" [8]—the people in Johannesburg suburbs whose wealthy lives are one long party). Ludman implies that Michelle is like her boyfried (an unselfish rebel) and her cousin (a cunning rebel). These altruistic Whites are presented for readers to identify with, but there are literally no Africans worth emulation. The turncoat, Joe, is reprehensible; the restaurant scullery maid, Beauty, is as inert as the vegetables she peels; the family housekeeper, Alice, is too blithely cheerful to comprehend anything resembling revolutionary change. Readers who are White will probably rest easy with Michelle, imagining little beyond a future South Africa that exploits cheap Black labor and marginalizes Black thinkers. Like Kugels, they are encouraged in this story to be "caring" but to avoid any real consideration of issues—issues that are urgent and highly relevant to the lives of Africans.

In the final analysis, whatever Ludman's motives, she tips the scale toward Whites: the White student demonstrators are heroic in the face of police batons, the older White women (the aunt and restauranteur) rescue Beauty and Alice from Soweto violence, the lawyer-uncle stands ready to offer prudent advice, and Cousin Clive assures Michelle that her boyfriend will suffer less at the hands of the police than Joe would have suffered. With this in mind, Clive tells Michelle to resist any disillusionment about Joe, the traitorous civil rights leader. But is it not a shock when a prominent Black intellectual saves himself by "squealing" on his anti-Apartheid compatriots? All Clive's explanation does is reinforce further the theme of White nobility in contrast to African disreputability.

While there is some credible detail in this novel about housing, schooling, and police brutality, the author generally sustains the notion of a White-over-Black hierarchy. She perpetuates stereotypes, as when she writes about how unreliable Black employees are: "The kaffirs, they just disappear, you know, not a word to anyone" (25). This is an Afrikaner speaking, but Ludman uses her plot line to validate the comment. She manipulates the action to suggest the inadvisability of collective action among Blacks—that is, unless some high-ranking Whites are on hand and in control.

THE SLAYER OF SHADOWS

Unlike *The Ink Bird* and *The Day of the Kugel*, Elana Bregin's novel is a post-election story.[3] *The Slayer of Shadows* seems to be saying, "We told you so. A Black government will be *no* government." At the center of this tale are gangs who terrorize virtually everyone. These Tsotsis (or "jakkals" as Bregin calls them) are in total control of a township and its surrounding territory. No counterforce is present despite the thousands who could function both as a governing body and a subduer of the young criminals: there are school teachers and authorities nearby, there is a rural population that comes into the township, there is the adult working class. But all these groups are portrayed as either accomplices in the sadistic acts of the "jakkals," or they remain passive. One can hardly imagine a more glaring statement about unreadiness for self-government.

Even a brief plot overview reveals how the narrative is conceived as a series of extreme exaggerations. The person referred to as "the slayer of shadows" is a mixed-race schoolteacher, Zach, who befriends a youngster called Sorrow. He re-names her Marinda and helps this eight-year-old and her grandmother survive. The rest of the family was massacred by the young criminals, who randomly burned houses and shot the fleeing residents, or else shot them first and then torched their homes. Marinda's mother was "necklaced" (burned to death with a burning tire encircling her body). According to this story, this anarchy exists because the anti-Apartheid movement was misconceived. The narrator, Marinda, explains: "We are less free than we ever were. . . . We are slaves to the . . . squabbling warlord packs that fight their territory battles around our home" (7). She describes the "jakkals" as the "scavengers," "robbing us and raping us as the whim inclines them . . ." (7). From this perspective, the post-election South Africa is an utter failure, although one wonders how a few months under Mandela can give the novelist such certainty on this matter. Using her young African mouthpiece she states that "the great Freedom Struggle, against our racist oppressors . . . [was] a just campaign. But soon, the power-greedy hijacked the Cause for their own ends. Few . . . feel any sense of liberation now" (7). Having virtually no government (now that the first democractic election has occurred), everyone is at the mercy of those who murder for pure amusement. The township is rotten to the core, a place with "fumes of excrement and decomposing corpses rising up to shroud it like poisoned smoke. The sight of its hideousness was terrible . . ." (27).

As this poisoned world sinks lower and lower, Marinda's life changes. She reaches her teens, her grandmother dies, and Zach and his pregnant wife let her live with them. But Zach is marked for execution. Only the talisman that Marinda has placed around his neck saves him (deflects the bullet). The jakkals then proceed to murder his wife, pull her unborn child from her womb, and hang the corpse on the door. When Zach finds her, the reader learns that "other atrocities too [were committed on this woman], but I shall not name them" (79). Bregin is keeping no secrets here; she has told us every sordid thing imaginable and her meaning is not obscure. She winds down the story with Marinda being raped, wounded, impregnated, and left to die. Zach is unable to locate her hiding place, and he becomes a lonely vagabond (the school having already fired him because his benevolence induced jakkal wrath). Ultimately Zach and Marinda find each other in a place far from the treacherous township ("the Jungle").

A theme running parallel to this Black-on-Black crime motif pertains to traditional African beliefs—especially ancestor worship and a belief in the supernatural. This is an ever-present element in the story, used to show how "primitive" thinking can be easily exploited by criminals. For example, the jakkals urge the assassination of Zach with this rationale: "The death of this arrogant Wizard would surely pacify our Ancestors. . . . 'Think what strong medicine we could make from his body parts!'" (68). Belief in sorcery "runs very deep in the Jungle," says the narrator (43), and this belief protects Zach for a time, because a Black man with bright yellow hair signals supernatural connections. But Zach is also labeled a wicked sorcerer, and on this assumption the rural people become a frenzied mob, attacking him and murdering the innocent woman that Zach is rescuing from thieves. As for Marinda, she has inherited the talents of a diviner and uses various amulets, but these methods prove to be useless. African beliefs are revealed as pointless at best and destructive at worst.

Zach functions as a failed Christ-figure—a teacher, a good Samaritan, a courageous model for the people—but no one has the power to overcome the monstrous evils unleashed in the post-election townships. At one point he asks a crowd, "Why let them abuse you? Band together and fight back when they accost you. Stand up for yourselves." Nothing, it seems, can stir this spineless population: "But nothing he said could arouse any spirit of rebellion in the people" (54). These are the Africans whose children died fighting in Soweto, whose labor unions merged into a formidable opposition force, whose leaders survived the horrors of Robben Island prison, and yet we are to believe Bregin's assertion that they had no "spirit of rebellion."

All this has the ring of a desperate voice—the voice of an aggrieved ruler warning about impending ruin. In her own extremist manner, Bregin joins Maartens and Ludman in maligning African self-determination and in promoting White rule.

A professional British educator, however, writing in an official library association journal, had only praise for this disturbing work. *The Slayer of Shadows*, wrote the book's reviewer, is a "gripping" and "powerful" novel for the young (Blaisdale 1996, 29).

* *

In the books critiqued here, there is such a topsy-turvy treatment of victims and victimizers that readers can miss entirely the price that the actual freedom struggle demanded of its participants. They will not know the sacrifices made by children like themselves: the tortures endured, the imprisonments, the endless interrogations, the flights into exile, the lengthy separations from family members. Instead the novels miseducate and leave untold the history of South Africa's steep, uphill journey toward democracy.

WORKS CITED

Blaisdale, Julie. 1996. Review of Elana Bregin's *The Slayer of Shadows*. *School Librarian* 44: 29.

Bregin, Elana. [1995] 1995. *The Slayer of Shadows*. Cape Town: Tafelburg. Reprint, London: Bodley Head.

Callinicos, Alex. 1988. *South Africa Between Reform and Revolution*. London, Chicago, Melbourne: Bookmarks.

Heale, Jay. 1996. Review of Maretha Maartens's *The Ink Bird*. In *From the Bushveld to Biko: The Growth of South African Children's Literature in English from 1907 to 1992 Traced through 110 Notable Books*, 37. Grabouw, S.A.: Bookchat.

Heale, Jay. 1994. *South African Authors & Illustrators*. Grabouw, S.A.: Bookchat.

Jones, Sean. 1993. *Assaulting Childhood: Children's Experiences of Migrancy and Hostel Life in South Africa*. Johannesburg: Witwatersrand University Press.

Ludman, Barbara. 1989. *The Day of the Kugel*. Cape Town: Maskew Miller Longman.

Maartens, Maretha. 1989. *The Ink Bird*. Cape Town: Tafelberg; Afrikaans ed. 1987; English ed. 1989. (Retitled *The Paper Bird: A Novel of South Africa*. Boston: Clarion/Houghton, 1991.)

O'Brien, Conor Cruise. 1987. "What Can Become of South Africa?" In *The Anti-Apartheid Reader: The Struggle Against White Racist Rule in South Africa*, ed. David Mermelstein, 430–473. New York: Grove Press.

Phelan, Carolyn. 1991. Review of Maretha Maartens's *The Ink Bird. Booklist*
    88: 137.

Seedat, Aziza. 1987. "Health in Apartheid South Africa." In *The Anti-
    Apartheid Reader: The Struggle Against White Racist Rule in South
    Africa.* Ed. David Mermelstein, 169–176. New York: Grove Press.

Seekings, Jeremy. 1993. *Heroes or Villains? Youth Politics in the 1980s.*
    Johannesburg: Ravan Press.

NOTES

1. Maretha Maartens was born in Bloemfontein and studied English and French at the University of the Orange Free State before training as a teacher at the University of Stellenbosch and as a nurse in Bloemfontein. She is active in youth programs in the Dutch Reformed Church (where her husband is a minister). She is the recipient of numerous book prizes. (See Jay Heale's *South African Authors & Illustrators*, 1994.)

2. Barbara Ludman has worked as a journalist in the United States and France, and in 1976 she married a South African in Paris and moved to South Africa. She has worked for many South African newspapers, and in 1989 (the date of this novel) she was the Arts Editor for the *Weekly Mail.*

3. Elana Bregin was born in Durban and graduated with a BA degree from the University of the Witwatersrand. She has been a dancer and a dance teacher, and she is a dedicated conservationist.

CHAPTER 4

Runaways, Forced Removals, Population Control

L abor rights, housing rights, and human rights have been denied the South African Black populations, and Apartheid's complicated laws have often tied these issues together. These laws restrained the influx of Blacks in terms of both localities and job markets. Black mobility was tightly controlled in order to maximize separation between the races, while maximizing the use of Black labor to enhance White profits.

Storytellers who bring these matters into the foreground typically employ a blame-the-victim approach, even while they insist they are using anti-Apartheid reference material in developing their expertise. For example, Lesley Beake claims her reliance on studies in *Growing Up in a Divided Society: The Context of Childhood in South Africa* (1986).[1] In developing her novel *The Strollers* (1987), Beake maintains that she was "generously allowed" to use materials later published in *Growing Up in a Divided Society*, but the fact remains that Beake's ideas about street squatters amd scavengers are quite alien to the ideas assembled in that anthology. Sandra Burman (the anthology's co-editor) (1986) writes that "phenomena of repression . . . have their instruments and their logic at the effective level of the family, of the immediate environment, of the most basic units of society" (7). This, she says, is the framework for gaining an understanding of "domination in South Africa." *The Strollers* contradicts this framework and substitutes the author's own explanation: the supposed pathology of Black people.

One would have to turn to the most ghoulish Dickensian tales to find the kind of child abusers Beake situates in Cape Town's Black communities. Her villains represent either African foolishness or malice, yet this is at odds with what authors Scharf et al. (1986) describe in *Growing Up* as the motivation and the "underlying structural dynamics which influence the 'strollers' existence." They state, "To confine oneself to the social pathology argument ignores . . . the material conditions in which certain classes find themselves . . . , [conditions] attributable to the policies of the ruling classes relating to social reproduction" (263–264). Beake is one of many authors who stick to the "social pathology argument," thereby turning the dynamics of Apartheid upside down and making the victims of that system the guilty parties. Beake's homeless children ("strollers") are abandoned, cast out, or physically injured by their Black parents. The policies of the White ruling regime are "offstage," and not presented in any cause and effect relationship to the blighted communities and lives.

THE RUNAWAYS' LIVES IN *THE STROLLERS*

Strollers are runaway children who live on their own, but do not join gangs. They can subsist as long as they can successfully beg, scavenge, steal, or devise scams (e.g., collect for nonexistent church charities). Beake's primary stroller-hero is Johnny, the eighth runaway in a township family of eight children. His seven brothers have been "swallowed up in the welter of people who no longer live at their home address" (2). With the exception of brother Abraham, we hear nothing more about Johnny's vanishing brethren. Abraham enters the tale because, as the leader of a criminally active gang, he has recruited some strollers for drug trafficking, and Johnny's group leader has informed on the gang when the police pick him up. Thus Koosie, the group leader, is banished to Johannesburg and Johnny takes charge.

The plot line moves Johnny around Cape Town: to a squatter community on Table Mountain, to the Saturday market stalls and the musicians who entertain customers, and finally to prison. This pilgrimage convinces him to return home, to revise his notion that a vagabond's life is a life of freedom. It has included only the freedom to get "high," to get sick, and to die (as is the fate of one TB-infected stroller in Johnny's group).

According to Beake's tale, an abusive Black community rather than an abusive White social system is at the bottom of the trouble. When the White system comes into view, we are assured that no one in that system is to blame. When Nelson, Johnny's stepfather, becomes unemployed due to a factory liquidation, we learn that "Nelson had meant well. Like Pa's dying, it hadn't been his fault" (5). When Johnny's school is depicted as chaotic, the overcrowding is treated as an unavoidable dilemma. It was all just a chronic problem of shortages: a shortage of teachers, a shortage of books. But the result is that Johnny is labeled in the official record as "a truant" and a "slow learner." Out of boredom and embarrassment, Johnny plays hookey and is then severely beaten by his stepfather. This leads to his decision to "stroll."

Instead of exposing Apartheid's culpability, Beake pinpoints anti-Apartheid activists as the destroyers of schools and families and as mindless troublemakers enticed by the excitement of revolution. They go on strike, close the school down intermittently, break windows, vandalize the newly painted school building, and generally create the bedlam that makes Johnny's teacher cry and his mother complain bitterly about the way "times are different" (3). "It's difficult," she says, "with the school sometimes out and the children who want to strike." For some inexplicable reason, neither Johnny nor his parents seem aware of the rationale behind the school strikes. They appear totally isolated from the democratic movement that is pushing for justice. They think there is some mysterious shortage of teachers, whereas the student activists undoubtedly know at least some of the realities, for example, that "there was one teacher for every 43 African children in comparison with one teacher for every 18 white children" (Chikane 1986, 339). Additionally, the monetary outlay was 1 Rand per African child in comparison with about 14.07 Rand for every White child (Chikane 1986, 339). The statistical breakdown for the 1982–83 period, as recorded by one journalist, was as follows:

Distribution of Resources According to Ethnicity in South African Schools, 1982–1983

	White	*Indian*	*Coloured*	*African*
Per Capita Expenditure (in South African Rands)	1,385	871	593	192
Teacher-Pupil Ratio	1:18	1:29	1:26	1:42
Underqualified Teaching Staff	3%	17%	59%	77%

Source: Adapted from statistics compiled by Graham Leach in *South Africa: No Easy Path to Peace* (Rev. ed. London: Methuen, 1987).

In relation to the stepfather's nonexistent schooling as a farm boy, Beake has Johnny ponder the problem as if Nelson himself is at fault:

> Other men came from the farms. Other men had some schooling. What was so different about Nelson? (3)

In fact, schooling for rural African children was a rarity. Nelson was not "different" because he had no schooling; he was ordinary.

In describing the other strollers in Johnny's group, Beake had an opportunity to bring some balance to the impression she is creating, but she rejects this opportunity. Ten-year-old Abel, Johnny's best friend, is instructed by his father to live on the streets and make money to donate to the family budget. He is depicted as an expendable item: "One less mouth [to feed], my Da always says" (6). Mesana is an eight-year-old girl whose father has died and whose mother has disappeared. (Apparently there are no relatives or friends in the family circle.) Spongasi and Nongosi are girls abandoned by their mother at the time when families were being "resettled" (i.e., forceably removed to a new location). Raymond destroyed so much school property that he was expelled. Andrew hated his home and no explanation is provided.

In contrast to all these dysfunctional urban people, the Africans remaining in the "Homelands" supposedly live an idyllic existence. Johnny tells of his grandparents in the Transkei—a grandmother who "wore a soft scarf made of pretty stuff," who was contentedly "looking after the fire, stirring the samp, plucking chickens on special days" (56).

> And I remember her hands were always busy with something, making things. She made some mats when I was there, out of plastic bags, all different colours and very pretty. . . . [O]ne day . . . he and his mother's mother were sitting outside the hut and she was content, with her long pipe in her hand, resting for once. Inside the hut, her husband, Johnny's own Baba, snored gently, and she smiled at Johnny, that smile of conspiracy that they shared sometimes about the old man. . . . (56)

Johnny becomes too tearful to continue his tale of grandmother's bucolic existence. Another child continues with a story of blissful rustic life.

This gives a largely false impression. Black people in rural South Africa were often at a point of near-starvation. They were removed from their original homes to dustbowl locations with no land to cultivate and no grazing land for cattle. In ranking general economic conditions, the authors of *The Surplus People* noted that "coloured and Indian people were favoured over African, urban people over rural people, industrial workers over agricultural workers. . . ." (Platzky and Walker 1985, 339).

Although Beake misleads as she describes rural life, she is apparently attempting a protest "statement" about homelessness. This seems clear from her treatment of how people view strollers: some onlookers fail to see them at all, some see them as a nuisance, but "didn't see *why* they were strolling" (67). Some wanted to provide soup kitchens and other material assistance, but "they didn't seem to understand, no, not at all, that the children were happy on the streets" (68). The novelist seems disapproving of callous onlookers, or people who are naive about the psychology of strolling, but Beake undermines her own compassionate theme by stereotyping Africans and "Coloureds" as criminals, fools, and hopeless alcoholics. Even the Rastamen—the musicians who befriend the strollers in the marketplace—have business dealings "of a highly illegal nature" (90). The "bergies" (the squatters on the mountain) are knife-wielding cutthroats. Abraham, Johnny's brother, is a long-established thief and drug dealer. With the exception of Johnny's mother, the primary Black characters seem to live on booze and hard drugs exclusively. Moreover, Abraham is the spiffily dressed clown who spends every other moment in front of the mirror. This is, supposedly, Beake's effort at comic relief:

> "Dark suits, man. That's what you wear to court, man."
>
> The only trouble was that Abraham's darkest suit was really deep purple. Perhaps that wasn't so bad, but the pale silver thread running through it tended to catch the eye. It had taken him a full hour to make up his mind if it was dark enough. . . .
>
> So in the end he had . . . toned down the effect somewhat with a pale orange shirt instead of the red one he usually wore with this outfit. . . . [H]e added . . . his diamond pin (so that the authorities would know they were dealing with a Person of Substance). (89)

This is one of many descriptions that turn Abraham into a stereotypic fool.

Abraham's criminal influence is also a problem for Johnny, and an elderly white man, Mr. Goldman, sends a lawyer to Johnny's aid.

When Johnny ultimately meets this benefactor, he begins to question the wisdom of the stroller lifestyle. As is usually the case in a Beake novel, a Black child/White adult connection becomes the means for arriving at a happy ending. In *The Strollers*, this means that Johnny returns to his mother and stepfather, and he takes the homeless eight-year-old girl with him. It is inferred that Johnny will stick to business at the hopelessly inadequate school, just as his mother sticks it out with his dispirited and violent stepfather.

By concentrating on this cast of largely dehumanized Blacks, the author substitutes Africans for the Apartheid government as the brunt of her social protest. These Africans express so little rationality that they can hardly function as agents of their own destiny. If they are not stumbling with drunkenness, they are irresponsibly carrying out acts of civil disobedience. The young dissidents are dismissed as gullible adolescents—as children caught "in the excitement of the speeches, the feeling of violence about to happen and the promise of something better" (60). If Beake had really heard the voices in the book she calls her source book—namely, *Growing Up in a Divided Society* (1986)—she would have created something quite different. But the novel she did write pleased book critics, as well as the prize-awarding jurors who awarded her the "Young Africa Award" in 1987.

Both Elwyn Jenkins (a South African professor of English) and British reviewer Val Booker critiqued Beake's work. Jenkins generalizes that "across some two dozen books on contemporary themes, it is possible to detect a pattern in the way black people are presented. . . . [I]n general black people are portrayed as good, caring, warm and loving" (Jenkins 1993, 137). What he fails to notice is that this pattern is intermittently true for Black children, but almost never true for Black adults. In fact, one of the most revealing trends in South African children's literature is the absence of normal, worthy Black adults. In *The Strollers*, the hero's stepfather beats him, his school teachers humiliate him, and Cape Town's adult vagrants are typically vicious and alcoholic. The homeless children do bond together harmoniously, but with the exception of Johnny's mother, the Black adults are a menace. Whites are introduced as the caregivers who intervene on behalf of the children.

Jenkins's praise also extends to the novel's attempt at comic relief. He applauds the humor in "this moving story"—humor centered on a "foppish gangster" (1993, 149). We see Beake's characterization of Johnny's boastful brother as a conventional and demeaning stereotype.

British reviewer Val Booker recommends *The Strollers* for children as young as nine years, and calls the novel "absorbing" and "well-written." "The author," we read, "manages to inject warmth and humour into Johnny's story which deserves the South African book prize it won" (Booker 1995, 107). Both reviewers, inexplicably, see life in the streets as a life where one finds "warmth." This interpretation sidesteps the grim injustices of Apartheid and the way Beake's novel glosses over them.

HOMELESSNESS IN *SERENA'S STORY*

In Beake's *Serena's Story* a girl is about to follow in her mother's foot-steps: she is to be sold into domestic service to pay off her mother's debts. All the parties in this transaction are the girl's own relatives, plus the Black drug traffickers who can successfully pressure people to give them their children. Gogo, the child's grandmother, hands over her granddaughter just as she had earlier sold her own child for thir-teen Rand per month to a White family. As this summary suggests, in 1990 Beake was still preoccupied with the Africans-are-dangerous theme. In contrast to these threatening characters, the protagonist's White savior (a police commissioner's widow) is down on her luck, but amply supplied with resilience, resourcefulness, and admirable values.

Serena is saved from a life of degradation and near-captivity by this widow—a woman so dependent on her husband and so ashamed of his violent career as Police Commissioner that she has submerged her mind in alcohol. She sleeps off her binges on the streets and is stum-bled upon by Serena, the teenager who is trying to escape from her impending sale to Beauty Mangele, a drug pusher. Once the widow sees this particular child in need, she decides to become her redeemer. She sets about rehabilitating herself, and when sober, wields some of the police power that belonged to her deceased spouse. Specifically, she is able to threaten the drug-dealing boss because she knows his police record.

The White crimes of Apartheid, plus any crimes by White drug traf-fickers, are kept offstage, while the Black underworld is paraded through the pages in graphic detail. This leaves the impression that no matter what faults are embedded in the Apartheid system, there is real-ly no alternative. With the exception of Serena, Beake introduces only Blacks who seem unfit for self-reliance, citizenship, or a role in good government. Their mean-spirited actions are a clear and present danger. Even though Serena's grandmother is selling her to a pusher in order to buy food and medicine for the remaining children, the real causes behind such grinding poverty (e.g., Apartheid's labor and "influx control" laws) remain largely unexposed. Similarly, prison conditions are brushed over lightly, even though Serena's mother, Thandi, is a drug user and is in jail throughout the tale. The reader is moved to first condemn Thandi because she "has gone with the rough men who live in Johannesburg" (4). But later we can feel glad about her release from prison and the guardianship that her family will enjoy at the hands of the White benefactor.

It is true that Beake exposes the hard lives of South African domestic workers (as when Beauty, Serena, and Thandi are all worn down by work days lasting from 6 A.M. to 9 P.M.). But this abusive system is overshadowed by another—the organized, marauding street children and by the pushers who use them as go-betweens. It is also overshadowed by the extortion rackets and by the kidnapping of children in order to use their labor as insurance against unpaid debts. All told, this tale puts Black-on-Black violence at the center of most scenes and avoids any truth telling about the poverty that characterizes urban South Africa. However, the actual conditions of township life need to be kept in mind.

The Realities of Township Poverty

We offer a few details about township poverty since Beake dwells upon its consequences without suggesting actual cause and effect relationships. For a child to become a captive (as in this story), there needs to be either extraordinary conditions or exceedingly depraved people. But when conditions are concealed, readers can only assume that it is very bad people at the heart of the problem—namely, the Black captors and child abusers. If we see almost nothing of township conditions, we fail to see Apartheid laws as the major causal force.

Studies of townships reveal calculated government policies behind the deprivation. At the most basic level this is because township regulation is connected to influx control. That is, Africans are intended to have only a migratory status in South African cities, to be "temporary sojourners" for the purposes of the labor force. The Bantustans or "Native" reserves are designated as the sites of African citizenship and nationhood, but in essence these are "catchment areas for the unemployed" and reserves for labor (Unterhalter 1987, 60). The gradual granting of "independence" or "self-rule" to Bantustans in 1976 was actually a facade used "to justify the denial of political rights, freedom of movement, and underdevelopment" (ibid, 24).

The level of underdevelopment varies among the townships and ranges from areas with some infrastructure to locations that lack water (except for infrequent public taps), electricity, sanitation, clinics, and schools. In some areas the shelter provided by the government consisted of a stand and four poles, plus a tent to erect over the stand (Platzky and Walker 1985, 345). Only when outside relief organizations stepped in and only when the international press publicized conditions—only then did "resettled" people receive the promised food and blankets. The high rates of disease caused by malnutrition and unsanitary living conditions (e.g., kidney diseases, cholera, and pneumonia) were largely ignored in Apartheid officialdom (ibid, 349).

Novelists are not journalists with a duty to expose such realities, but when storytellers contrive characters with extreme behavior, they are implying an underlying rationale. By ignoring the material conditions of existence, they can make a false psychological condition appear plausible. This kind of storytelling serves the political agenda of Apartheid. It is a narrative technique used also in novels about forced removals.

FORCED RELOCATIONS IN *A SUDDEN SUMMER*

Dianne Hofmeyr's *A Sudden Summer* (1987) centers on the connections between schooling, housing, and labor.[2] The government's policy of "influx control" meant that Africans, "Coloureds," and Asians were tolerated in locations designed as "White areas" only as long as they were there to meet perceived labor needs. When those needs changed, the government undertook programs of forced removal to resettle the unwelcome population in new areas. Education for Black children had no rationale except in relation to those same perceived labor needs.

Hendrik Frensch Verwoerd (Prime Minister from 1958 to 1966) stated the educational policy for "Natives":

Native education should be controlled in such a way that it should be in accord with the policy of the state. . . . If the native in South Africa today in any kind of school in existence is being taught to expect that he will live his adult life under a policy of equal rights, he is making

a big mistake. . . . There is no place for him in the European community above the level of certain forms of labour. (quoted in Thompson
1995, 196)

Hofmeyr's novel gives implicit support to Verwoerd's philosophy,
while also attempting to sound humane. She does not object to the
removal policy. She only contrives a plot line in which one "Coloured"
family can circumvent its implications. To bring about this happy ending, Hofmeyr must contradict her own sermons about keeping "apartness" (i.e., Apartheid) intact.

Mary, the "Coloured" protagonist, has a White acquaintance,
Corina, who is definitely "apart." Most of the novel is an account of
Corina's romance with David, a nonconforming art student who is a
paragon of friendliness, wisdom, and artistic sensibility. He is also the
one carrying the author's messages about removal policy and about
"Coloureds" as a race apart from Whites—a group with its own sepa-
rate destiny and built-in survival skills. While Corina wants to help
Mary's family (squatters in the sand dunes), she nonetheless absorbs
David's views about forced removals and how they are perfectly in line
with laws of nature.

Corina's observations bring into the story actual government initiatives vis-à-vis removals. For example, when she sees a headline about
a new uprising in the squatter camp called Crossroads, we know the
year is 1985 and that the government is once again trying to demolish
this camp that originated in the mid-1970s. When residents in
Crossroads resisted removal, the police crackdown left eighteen people
dead and more than 230 injured (Platzky and Walker 1985, xxvi).
Corina believes that her family members should be discussing this, but
her immediate concern is the "Coloured" satellite community that sits
"like a tickbird on the back of Gordon's Bay" (3). Temperance Town
is "a little cluster of 'coloured' houses," the homes of the "charwomen
[who] came bumping down the aisle" of the bus Corina rides to
school. These women are the "tickbirds"—the labor force that serves
the middle-class Whites. They are scheduled for removal to an outly-
ing area called Macassar, but since Mary's father is a fisherman, he is
trying to escape the removal ultimatum and thereby keep his independent means of employment. First he secludes his family in a forest-
ed area (where his shack burns down), and then among the sand dunes.
Mary's meeting with Corina threatens the family's fugitive status, and
its safety becomes a problem for Corina and her father. But first the

reader receives lessons on the removal issue by way of Hofmeyr's use of birds as metaphors.

At this point David plays the role of reliable narrator, counseling Corina about things in their "right place." He tells her that it is a mistake to help a blind "jackass penguin" that has washed ashore. He seems to know what is "best" for a stranded bird, even as he knows what is "best" for "Coloured" squatters. He persuades Corina that just as birds are rightly finding their way home by means of natural forces, so it is natural that "Coloureds" be entirely under government control. David says: "Come, we must leave it [the 'jackass penquin'] . . . . He'll be fine. He'll cope without you" (24). Corina tells David about the squatters in the dunes, and he has a similar reply when she asks "Do you think we could help them?"

> "No, not really. They'll have to move to Macassar eventually."
> "But surely there must be somewhere in Gordon's Bay where they can live. Do you think that I should speak to my father?"
> "I don't know whether one should interfere with their lives. You don't even know Mary's family!" (49)

Corina and David locate Mary, but when Mary hesitates before approaching them, David repeats his advice: "Perhaps you should have just left things as they were. . . . Come Corina. Let's leave her. We're just causing her embarrassment" (50). The Whites in this story have no qualms about government interference in Black lives, but suddenly David is worried about "interfering" with Mary's troubles. Corina listens and passes on his "wisdom" by telling Mary how she should think about some nesting swallows: "[A]nimals and birds know instinctively what's right for them . . . and humans shouldn't interfere" (45).

Besides allusions to tickbirds, penguins, and swallows, Hofmeyr includes a discussion of the Red-chested Cuckoo. There is no particular logic in this selection of the Cuckoo other than its use as a commentary on migrant living. Corina instructs Mary about this bird, explaining about the Cuckoo's travels from Central Africa. Mary then reads from the bird dictionary:

> [T]he Cuckoo lays its egg in the nest of the Cape Robin. The Cuckoo chick evicts the young of its foster parents, by carrying them on its back to the lip of the nest and rolling them over the edge. (45)

Corina exclaims, "How dreadful!" but then invokes David's philosophy: "I suppose that's just instinctive behavior" (45).

Biological determinism seems implicit in all the novel's bird lore. Nature dictates a "survival of the fittest" program with respect to lodgings and all other group arrangements. In short, it is not surprising that "Coloured" satellite communities are nudged out of their "nests" as the stronger White groups require. Scientific racism would say that it is inevitable.

In *A Sudden Summer*, living conditions are clearly intolerable in the dunes because of storms, winds, and lack of water. But there is no description of how similarly intolerable life is likely to be in new townships and "Homelands"—places like Temperance Town and Macassar, places that David accepts as the inevitable and rightful home sites for people of color. Under the Group Areas Act (1950), "Coloureds" and Asians, as well as Africans, were forced to live in designated zones, and these areas were often completely undeveloped. They had "mud, clapboard, or corrugated iron buildings, with earth latrines. . . ." They "stood on tiny plots of land and were served by water from infrequent taps along the unpaved paths and roads" (Thompson 1995, 170). All we learn from the novel is that satellite communities (such as the one near Corina's home) included houses without electricity, and that deprivation didn't dampen anyone's spirits! "[The charwomen were] laughing and shrieking at the back of the bus," and "chuckling and waving at the driver as he pulled away" (3).[3]

While shanty town realities remain hidden in Hofmeyr's narrative, so too are educational realities undisclosed. For example, to give the story a happy ending, Hofmeyr assures the reader that Mary's fondest wish will come true: she will be allowed to remain in her "Coloured" school. (This is assumed since the family has been rescued by a government official, a man who offers the family lodgings and work at his "bait and tackle" shop.) But even if this family escapes the forced removal through these special circumstances, what makes us think that the "Coloured" school will remain in Gordon's Bay? Who would be left to attend it after everyone has been shipped off to Macassar? To be realistic, we must conclude that this plot line leaves Mary with *no schooling.*

In the 1960s, the government had taken control of Asian and "Coloured" schools, just as it had taken control of schools for Africans under the Bantu Education Act of 1953. This act had essentially closed down non-government schools, schools the Apartheid regime viewed as carriers of "dangerous, alien ideas" (Thompson 1995, 196). In the government-run Black and "Coloured" schools, classes were over-crowded, teachers were poorly paid, and textbooks taught only the government-prescribed racial policy. Even if Mary had ended up with a "Coloured" school to attend, she would have been subjected to an abusive, racist curriculum. Moreover, in Hofmeyr's novel "Coloured" education is treated with skepticism, since Mary is depicted as less than bright. She has accepted Corina's offer of friendship only because she is doing poorly on exams and hopes to boost her grades with a special project. Since the reader hears nothing about the actual conditions in schools for "Coloureds," they can only assume that Mary is either lazy or mentally "slow."

By the end of this tale, the girls face a future that conforms to Prime Minister Verwoerd's policies for Black education and Black labor. That is, Corina's White South African family will continue demanding "Coloured" servants and set the terms in accordance with its own interests. It will manipulate housing and schooling arrangements in relation to its perceived labor needs. On the other hand, Mary must not think she will have equal rights. She warrants, perhaps, a helping hand, but only within the parameters of the unjust Apartheid laws.

* *

Forced removals affected at least four million people since the Apartheid regime gained control in 1948. This enormous number did not arouse any noticeable international intervention since population control was integral to the Apartheid exploitation of labor, and the capitalist world did not, apparently, resist capitalist development under any conditions.[4] At least in the African context, international opposition was not forthcoming, despite the reality that "few black South Africans [were left untouched] by the harassment, domestic upheaval, confusion and poverty which are the consequences of the [forced removal] policy" (Unterhalter 1987, 1).

As the Apartheid government loosened some of its hardline policies in the late 1980s (after the world raised belated objections), "influx control" was superceded by a policy of "orderly urbanization." The pass laws were scrapped and the government "direct[ed] people towards specified growth points . . . where jobs and housing were available" (Leach 1987, 94). But some critics saw this as "influx control in different clothing" (94). The key issue remained: Would public policy continue as a servant of a white supremacist ideology?

A corollary question could be posed in the field of education: Will a democratic education policy evolve from a children's literature that embraces the notion of race separation and race hierarchy? This remains an unanswered question since a race separation in children's books is still either taken for granted or blithely denied.

WORKS CITED

Beake, Lesley. 1987. *The Strollers*. Cape Town: Maskew Miller Longman.

Beake, Lesley. 1990. *Serena's Story*. Cape Town: Maskew Miller Longman.

Booker, Val. 1995. Review of Lesley Beake's *The Strollers*. *School Librarian* 43: 107.

Burman, Sandra. 1986. "The Contexts of Childhood in South Africa: An Introduction." In *Growing Up in a Divided Society: The Contexts of Childhood in South Africa*, eds. Sandra Burman and Pamela Reynolds, 1–15. Johannesburg: Ravan Press.

Chikane, Frank. 1986. "Children in Turmoil: The Effects of the Unrest on Township Children." In *Growing Up in a Divided Society: The Contexts of Childhood in South Africa*, eds. Sandra Burman and Pamela Reynolds, 333–344. Johannesburg: Ravan Press.

Coles, Robert. 1986. *The Political Life of Children*. Boston, New York: The Atlantic Monthly Press.

Hofmeyr, Dianne. 1987. *A Sudden Summer*. Cape Town: Tafelberg.

Jenkins, Elwyn. 1993. *Children of the Sun: Selected Writers and Themes in South African Children's Literature*. Johannesburg: Ravan Press.

Leach, Graham. 1987. *South Africa: No Easy Path to Peace*. Rev. ed. London: Methuen.

Platzky, Laurine and Cherryl Walker. 1985. *The Surplus People: Forced Removals in South Africa*. Johannesburg: Ravan Press.

Scharf, Wilfried, Marlene Powell and Edgar Thomas. 1986. "Strollers—Street Children of Cape Town." *In Growing Up in a Divided Society: The Contexts of Childhood in South Africa*, eds. Sandra Burman and Pamela Reynolds, 262–287. Johannesburg: Ravan Press.

Thompson, Leonard. 1995. *A History of South Africa*. Rev. ed. New Haven and London: Yale University Press.

Unterhalter, Elaine. 1987. *Forced Removal: The Division, Segregation and Control of the People of South Africa*. London: International Defence and Aid Fund for South Africa; Canon Collins House.

NOTES

1. Lesley Beake was educated at Rhodes University and UNISA. She has been a teacher and has traveled widely in Namibia, Hong Kong, the Persian Gulf, and Britain (including Scotland, her birthplace). Her books have been published in Germany, the Netherlands, the United States, Great Britain, and France.

2. Dianne Hofmeyr grew up in Gordon's Bay, the setting for this novel, and moved from Stellenbosch to Johannesburg in 1982. She has been an art teacher, and her novels have won several awards.

3. These jovial images are entirely at odds with the bitter, insightful impressions of young Africans. One thirteen-year-old commented: "They love us to be 'tribal,' the rich whites who come here. They throw their rand at us, if only we'll become Zulus and Bantus and Xhosas once again, and stop bothering them with our demands to be part of *their* country! They'd like us to disappear into the bush, but any time they whistle, to come out and get right to work, doing their shoveling and laying their bricks and lifting anything that's too heavy for them and sweeping their streets and carrying their garbage." (See Robert Coles's *The Political Life of Children*, p. 216.)

4. In the time frame of Hofmeyr's novel, the foreign investment by the West in South Africa was approximately $25 billion. U.S. involvement was enormous: $2.5 billion worth of direct investment, $3.9 billion worth of bank loans, $7.6 billion worth of shares in companies, and exports totaling $2 billion. Economist Raymond Lotta concluded in 1985 that U.S. economic expansionism and Apartheid "require each other." (See "The Political Economy of Apartheid and the Strategic Stakes of Imperialism," *Race and Class* XXVII: 2 [1985], p. 18.)

CHAPTER 5

The First Democratic Election: Right-Wing Fears in Post-Election Fiction

O ne election does not create a new society," writes historian G. H. L. LeMay (1994, 261). Or, to put it differently, "When South Africa stepped through the looking glass, it did not emerge in Wonderland" (Waldmeir 1997, 283). To expect a perfect transition between the "Old" and "New" regimes would scarcely be realistic. But there are novels dating from the mid-1990s that call into question even the wisdom and legitimacy of an ex-Apartheid nation. This is our concern in this chapter. While the stories we cover here bring Black and White people together, the election of 1994 is presented with skepticism or even ridicule. In Dennis Bailey's *Thatha* (1994),[1] a Black electoral candidate is characterized as corrupt, vicious, and hypocritical, as well as a sex crime offender against his own daughter. In Lawrence Bransby's *Outside the Walls* (1995), the election is described as a rigged affair—a political mockery that gave advantages to Blacks. Mandela's picture is pasted on every other lamppost, and the novel's young protagonist takes every opportunity to mock Mandela and Black voters in general. In Bransby's *The Boy Who Counted to a Million* (1995), the ANC and Inkatha political parties are maligned as equally ludicrous or inhumane. As we consider the details in the Bailey and Bransby books, we will see a mixed set of emotions and agendas. Democracy is accepted as an ideal, but not as a tenable form of political practice.

THATHA

In this novel, the atrocities of Apartheid are a thing of the past and sit-

uated well "off stage." "On stage" action highlights the way good
White people are restraining the sinister acts of a Black candidate and
his political operatives. By making this reprehensible candidate
(Joshua Rabede) a one-time prisoner at the Robben Island prison (the
"home" of Mandela for twenty-seven years), the novelist is associating
the freedom fighter prisoners with a high level of corruption and
wrongdoing. According to this story, Black politicians talk a good line,
but it is all "show."

Thatha (the daughter of Rabede) is kidnapped along with her
boyfriend, Mark Stanford. She suspects her father's complicity in this
act, believing that "kidnapping was not the style of her father's political opponents" (7). She rightly surmises that her father's intention was
to stir up interest in his electoral campaign. While making these deduc-
tions, she is careful to conceal from Mark her own tragic past—her
rape and pregnancy at the hands of her father.

Arguably, it is the Reverend Eddie Stanford, Mark's father, who is
supposed to come across as the real hero. He is the one managing the
region's Independent Electoral Commission, the group that monitors
voting stations and campaign tactics. At every stage we see the election
threatened by cheating, unreasonable labor disputes, and the criminality of people like candidate Rabede. As for the Reverend and the
town's public officials, they are the now reformed democracy-lovers
who will save South Africa from brutish Black politicians. These new
converts to one person/one vote elections will try to make the best of
it by holding Black crime in check. Some allusions are made in the narrative to the crimes of Apartheid officialdom, but the major threat is
Thatha's father—a "wild" man, a person who lusts for his own twelve-
year-old and is infuriated when discovering the intrusion of school
counselors in his affairs. He pummels Thatha with his fists, and is only
restrained by the intervention of his wife. In efforts to protect this violent man, Thatha leads people to suspect that a friend's slain brother
was her rapist. This is pure fabrication, but it gives the friend
(Thulani) a chance to serve as the author's mouthpiece. Even though
his family has suffered enormously, Thulani understands that Whites
are no more to blame for South Africa's troubles than Blacks. He
speaks of the crimes committed by freedom fighters (the "comrades"):
"Before there were people's courts, the comrades got away with a lot
of rough stuff in the townships because no-one would cooperate with
the police" (82). And he adds, "Apartheid can't be blamed for all
oppression" (42). This idea of shared guilt is especially noticeable in

scenes where the grotesque Rabede makes political speeches. Readers know by now that he has raped and impregnated his daughter, so his speeches to charm the electorate seem highy offensive as well as hypocritical. He addresses reporters at a press conference:

> The pressures are great on any family that aspires to public life, and when my daughter was abducted from school four days ago I was tempted to go back to cattle-herding. When your family falls victim to the more villainous elements opposed to the democratic process, one begins to wonder whether the price is worth paying. . . . As an ex-Robbin Islander I want to affirm that it is. As a political leader returned from exile I want to affirm that it is. . . . Finally, . . . it is my sincere hope that in a more politically free and just dispensation, people will not have to resort to such extremism in order to make their voices heard. (111, 114)

These syrupy words are spoken only minutes before Rabede's criminality is exposed and he is forced to flee in his Mercedes. Meanwhile, Thatha continues her inner struggle:

> Terror held her in its grip. She was afraid of her father's unbridled brutality, fearing most for her mother at home with her [Thatha's] child. She was afraid of Sipho [her brother], of what he might do once his anger erupted. (123)

Thatha objects to Mark Stanford's insistence that all this corruption be brought into the open. But it is doubtful that the book's White readers will object. The Stanfords stand for truth-seeking and other virtues, whereas Black culpability is too pervasive to compel even the slightest sympathy. Even the character of Thulani's martyred brother is diminished by the assertion that he was drunk when the police arrested him as a security risk.

Besides these one-sided characterizations, Bailey brings specific political debates into his narrative. For example, Sipho tells his sister that he is disillusioned by Rabede's tactic of infiltrating opposition parties. His father, he says, is conducting sabotage, "if not outright annihilation of all opposition" (57). As his father's son, he feels he must join the saboteurs, but Thatha disagrees:

"If APP can't fight this election without doing this sort of thing it doesn't deserve to win. . . . Is that what you sacrificed your education for? Is that kind of democracy any better than apartheid?"

"Anything is better than apartheid, Thatha."

"No it's not, Sipho." (57)

Thatha explains to Sipho about "that kind of democracy": "It's just a more democratic form of oppression and you know it" (57). This exchange suggests that under Black leadership, the type of democracy that is to be expected is the type that will only tarnish democracy. Rabede and the APP are offered to the reader as a case in point.

The strategy is to make young Blacks serve as the author's mouthpiece. Besides Thulani and Thatha, we have Kletho, a character making the case for non-involvement. Kletho is admired as a non-political type, and his worldview comes to the reader through his comments to reporters: "Even after this election, young people will still be refugees in their own home town" (120). He shares lines from one of his poems: "Now all may vote who will mop up the tears?/Now children have rights who will pay back their stolen years/ . . . Or is death our only hope of liberation? . . ." (121). Is this saying that human rights are at best deceptive or unachievable? Will people be able to relate to each other freely only in death? Kletho expressed this deadbeat attitude earlier when he stood outside the township's burning office building: "What do elections and fires have in common? . . . They terrify widows, make children orphans, and bring us grief" (39). Since when do democratic elections "terrify"? Is Kletho's cynicism a desirable position from which to shape a New South Africa?

Characters who sneer at elections also inhabit Lawrence Bransby's *Outside the Walls*.[2] Bransby offers some sympathy for impoverished Blacks, but his storyline presents no options for them other than the reception of "hand-outs" from Whites. In the White teenage hero, there is a change from callous observer to generous helper as squatter camps move into his vicinity.

OUTSIDE THE WALLS

Mandela's smile beams from lamppost posters as seventeen-year-old John visits his mother's voting station. As John observes election day crowds, he is full of witticisms about the ever-present electoral corruption. Bransby sets up John as an "unreliable" narrational voice at this point, so to some degree his mockery is to be viewed ironically. But even so, there is no counterstatement when John's snide remarks about Mandela are offered as a recurring pattern throughout the book. Nor does the author provide an effective storytelling technique to counteract the direct anti-Black insinuations. For example, John comments: "I mean they're handing temporary voting cards to anyone who asks for them—like suckers. If you're black and look vaguely over sixteen—PRESTO!—you get a card and can vote!" (8).

In the first two chapters John ridicules the election as "THE Great Grey Green Greasy Election" and whines about being "not really the Politically Correct Colour just at this moment. Just a shade on the light side, I believe" (13, 14). But John is stressed out, so we must consider the source. He is frantically suppressing his pain over his father's desertion, but after some healing, John turns from his role as a smart-ass commentator to the role of a more reliable reporter. He relates straightforwardly how Black squatters have established themselves in an area adjacent to White suburbia.

Bransby contrives a conventional "change-of-heart" story, yet he also presents his own interpretation of what is happening in South Africa. In the end John will be slightly less angry with his parents, but this is because several squatters have become like family to him. One squatter in particular, Philip, becomes like a surrogate father, and his wise counsel helps John come to terms with his fractured home life. But in his political analysis, Bransby sees only a Black "problem," whether it is Black political parties, Black squatters, or Black thieves.

In the novelist's analysis, it is the ANC and the Inkatha party that have produced the shanty towns and camps. As narrator, John describes the evolution of this problem:

> The squatter community grew by one or two each day, straggling in from the outlying areas where starvation or political fighting drove them. . . . Philip's shack became our [John and Gweneth's] hideout. . . . We ate putu with our fingers and samp and beans with the same spoon and heard about the killings in the rural areas, the attacks of ANC and Inkatha hit-squads which everyone claimed didn't exist. (104, 105)

These "hit-squads" are only one part of the chain of violence. The squatters steal cars and livestock, break into suburban houses, and are eventually loaded into police vans as demolition teams cart away their jerry-built shacks. In all this there is no clue as to real cause and effect relationships. Why the starvation? Why the hit-squads? Why are Black political parties being mutually destructive? Has a White Apartheid government had anything to do with civic and rural problems? Was the South African government itself the most dangerous "hit-squad," even during the post-1990 electoral negotiations? Historian T. R. H. Davenport (1998) recounts the National Party's complicity in political murders:

> The government consistently denied ANC charges that there had been, and still was, a 'third force' whose role was to eliminate targeted resistance leaders, yet there had been an escalation of unexplained political murders during the 1980s, sometimes sensationally linked to security force activity. (33)

Leonard Thompson (1995) confirms the government/Inkatha collusion: "[S]enior military and police officers exacerbated Zulu conflicts by supplying Inkatha with arms and money and by turning a blind eye to Inkatha atrocities or even provoking them" (247). Readers of Bransby's story are left with no accurate information on the "security force" involvement in violence. Instead, Bransby gives them grotesque descriptions of Black people. For example, Philip's son, Vukani, is repeatedly referred to as "lizard-faced" (72, 103), and an elderly woman who becomes part of Philip's extended family is treated as a muttering, grunting hag. As she tends to the cooking we see her in these terms: "She crouched and blew on the flames, her wrinkled breasts hanging like leather thongs from her chest" (100).

Bransby's other novel from 1995, *The Boy Who Counted to a Million*, is about a closely knit suburban family, but in other ways we see similarities with *Outside the Walls*. The election is still in the campaigning stage and it remains a problematic event to this novelist.

THE BOY WHO COUNTED TO A MILLION

Pre-election violence on the part of Blacks is in the foreground in this award-winning story. This material gives Bransby a chance to make various editorial points. He suggests, for example, that Blacks understand little about the democratic process in which they are about to participate. Their confusion results, apparently, from political inexperience, from the murderous behavior of Black factions (especially the ANC and the Inkatha Freedom Party), and from mental backwardness in general. Additionally, Bransby implies that the White population can only hope to bring about some "damage control" and fend off threats to their own homes. With these motifs, the author is able to introduce the Black "brute" and the minstrel-like "clown." The final impression is that Blacks are unready for self rule, yet are aggressively muscling their way into the White sphere, the sphere of constitutional government. The story line amplifies these messages when the son of an Anglican minister, Matthew, watches his father rush to the scene of each new Black-on-Black murder and offer spiritual comfort. This clergyman can only sigh with frustration as he embarks on each of these missions. He sees the ANC/Inkatha conflict as mindless faction-alism, as well as a prediction of the chaos that South Africa will expe-rience under the one person/one vote policy. There is not a word about what kinds of issues are of concern to either ANC members or the fol-lowers of Inkatha's Buthelezi. Both organizations are counterproduc-tive at best, treacherous at worst. They have no political convictions and are murdering innocent men, women, and children out of pure malice. They beat and kill school teachers, burn down schools, and force young people to attend invidious political meetings. The call by African party officials to meet and plan collective action receives no credible description. How could Blacks possibly know how to conduct a democratic gathering! In short, Blacks are disallowed any meaning-ful role in the world of political debate.

What we see of African political engagement is laughable. Simon, the Black housekeeper's husband, plays the fool by swinging like a pendulum between the parties he sees as his choices. Throughout the campaign period, he acts as if his brain is overtaxed. When young Matthew asks if he plans to vote, he exclaims:

> "Vote!" . . . "Too much!" . . . "Too much!" he repeated.
>
> "Are you going to vote ANC?" Matthew asked, nodding towards the photograph of Mandela.
>
> "Matts, I am a Zulu. I vote for Buthelezi. IFP—" (34)

Later Matthew and Simon again discuss the election, and Simon asks for the child's advice as he describes the campaigning:

> "A man from the ANC, he come here to see me. He say there are twenty-eight million Blacks in this country and we must all vote ANC so Mandela can be president."

"What did you say?"

"I just keep quiet, Mattu, and I smile. There is too much killing here, ANC, INKATHA, tsotsis—all the time! . . . If you INKATHA, ANC want to kill you, burn your house. If you ANC, watch out for INKATHA!— they come in the night. All the time!" He shook his head sadly then laughed. "I don't say nothing! Maybe I vote DP! Maybe NP! Who knows? What you say?" (59)

After Simon is assassinated, it is implied that an ANC member (a caftan-clad Muslim) is the one who commits the crime.

While this Black chaos is underway, the author builds in a secondary plot about the blood baths in France in World War I. Knowing this history apparently advances Matt's maturation process. When Matthew's great-grandfather moves in with the family in his ninety-seventh year, he helps Matt overcome his childish tendency to glorify war. He recounts his own participation in one of World War I's cruelest contests. Matthew gains a new desire to build a unified South Africa, but he has no experience with viable Black/White relations. The boy's knowledge of Blacks is only a knowledge of servants. And Bransby's kind of servants are happy in servitude and generally addlebrained.

For example, Elizabeth, the housekeeper/cook, is a devout Christian, but a foolish one. She is apparently incapable of anything much beyond her standard response to the day's challenges: "I have been spared for another day" (18). Her ten-year-old son has been allowed to stay with her since his school has been burned down by marauding ANC or Inkatha forces. Her husband, Simon, lives behind the shop that he owns—that is, until the shop is also torched. How this family can be so perpetually happy with this arrangement is never explained—an arrangement that forces the husband to live alone, that separates him from his family, that is so unprofitable that Elizabeth can expect no life other than that of a live-in scrub woman. Nonetheless, Simon is appallingly happy-go-lucky and stops smiling only when he is brutally stabbed to death. His Christian angels have, it seems, abandoned him.

The ferocity of this act points to the wartime climate of the period Bransby chooses as his setting. The point needs to be made that Apartheid was a war against the Black population, even if Bransby chooses to present conflicts as Black-on-Black events. Narrative material that would have been pertinent to Apartheid's warring history was certainly available to the storyteller, but remained unused. Instead

Bransby makes much of the authenticity in his treatment of World War I. In an "Author's Note," he tells of his conscientious research: "All references to the battle of Delville Wood have been loosely based on the recorded experiences of men who were there. . . ." (unpaged). What about the people who were there in the Apartheid vs. African war? Would the reader have gained some awareness of what was going on if the novelist had studied the words of people like Nelson Mandela, Thabo Mbeki, and Oliver Tambo? *Those* words would have shown Apartheid's war against Blacks as a project that almost irretrievably fractured Black/White relations. They would have touched upon the real history of South African children.

Bringing authenticity to recent South African history would have entailed depictions of Black children who lived across the great Apartheid divide—outside the secure, protected, affluent world that Matthew enjoyed with his parents and servants. Matthew counts to a million in his effort to fathom what his great-grandfather has told him about the ten million who died in World War I. But what did Matthew need to know about the African casualties since the Apartheid regime commenced in 1948? What did he need to know about destitution in the "Homelands," about detainees never accounted for after their imprisonment, about the enormous child death rate attributed to malnutrition?

Some of these children were interviewed by Fiona McLachlan (1986), a practicing attorney in Johannesburg and a researcher for the international children's rights organization, Defense for Children International. One child, for stealing clothes, was detained for thirteen months without a trial, without bail, without counsel, without food except for porridge and bread, without the right to see his mother (345). Another child, a fifteen-year-old, was detained for just fourteen days, but came away with extreme mental damage. He no longer knew where he was, he wandered off aimlessly, he muttered over and over: "Let them kill me, they must finish me off." He had become unrecognizable to his mother (345).

In spinning out a story about the Apartheid war, an author such as Bransby would have had to face the reality of the "Emergency Regulations" passed in 1985—regulations that had many negative connections with children. For example,

• Parents and relatives were not informed of the child's detention or whereabouts.

• A prisoner could have indefinite detention with no right of representation for the detainee.

• A child's parents and relatives had no visitation rights.

• No inspection of juvenile cells was provided for—inspections by outsiders such as medical and legal professionals.

• Minor children could be subjected to lengthy interrogations with no one serving as counsel or guardian.

• Solitary confinement could be used with child detainees.
(McLachlan, 354)

Of course a novelist need not take account of such abuses. Storytellers have innumerable choices and Bransby comments understandably in his "Author's Note" that he used "creative license wherever necessary" (unpaged) as he reconstructed World War I. The first democratic election in 1994 had much to do with warfare, and Bransby could have combined his interest in *that election* with an interest in the *relevant war*. We cannot second guess the creative process, but we can say that when a writer misrepresents the 1994 election (as in Bransby's case) it is not surprising that the whole context and meaning of that election are kept well out of sight.

But the book critics were well-pleased. In announcing the book as the 1996 award winner chosen by the South African Institute for Library and Information Science, the annotator highlighted Bransby's ability to excel "at portrayals of both family relationships and moral choices" (Bookbird 1997, 50). The critic saw the juxtaposition of World War I and "strife-torn Kwa-Zulu Natal before the 1994 democratic elections" as a successful artistic maneuver—a way to indicate that both child and great-grandfather had to face up to "senseless violence." This unqualified praise shows something of the White solidarity among those who write, publish, and reward books that stereotype Africans. It suggests that well-meaning educators sometimes keep in their line of vision only White children, no matter how important the subject at hand may be to Black children.

* *

One of the blind spots in these "election" novels is the way the novelists ignore the African willingness to be conciliatory during the negotiation period from 1991–1994. Throughout the whole time, as Leonard Thompson (1995) reports, "Right-wing Whites continued to assassinate black politicians" (248). But in spite of this pressure from extremists, the ANC acquiesced in a compulsory power-sharing arrangement in the National Cabinet— "a major concession to . . . white South Africans" (250). And, ironically, it was a South African Communist Party secretary-general, Joe Slovo, who persuaded the ANC to yield to National Party demands for the honoring of contracts of civil servants. This concession (ill-advised in our view) ensured the continuing influence of a largely Afrikaner bureaucracy in the structure of the New South Africa (249).

In a word, the realities of the first democratic election are not projected in South African children's novels. The true story of that election is one of leaders at the top going to almost any lengths to avert a civil war. A deep commitment to this peace-with-justice theme reverberates through Mandela's inaugural address:

> Never, never, and never again shall it be that this beautiful land will again experience the oppression of one by another. (quoted in Thompson 1995, 255)

WORKS CITED

Bailey, Dennis. 1994. *Thatha*. South Africa: Heinemann.

Bransby, Lawrence. 1995. *The Boy Who Counted to a Million*. Cape Town: Human and Rousseau.

Bransby, Lawrence. 1995. *Outside the Walls*. Oxford: Oxford University Press.

Davenport, T. R. H. 1998. *The Transfer of Power in South Africa*. Cape Town: David Philip Publishers.

LeMay, G. H. L. 1994. *The Afrikaners: An Historical Perspective*. Oxford: Blackwell Publishers.

McLachlan, Fiona. 1986. "Children in Prison." In *Growing Up in a Divided Society: The Contexts of Childhood in South Africa,* eds. Sandra Burman and Pamela Reynolds, 345–359. Johannesburg: Ravan Press.

Bookbird 35: 50. Review of Lawrence Bransby's *The Boy Who Counted to a Million.*

Thompson, Leonard. 1995. *A History of South Africa.* Rev. ed. New Haven and London: Yale University Press.

Waldmeir, Patti. 1997. *Anatomy of a Miracle: The End of Apartheid and the Birth of the New South Africa.* New York and London: W.W. Norton and Co.

NOTES

1. Dennis Bailey lives in Pietermaritzburg and is a teacher, youth worker, father of three sons, priest, and current director of an international reproductive health NGO.

2. Lawrence Bransby graduated from the University of Natal and won a scholarship to complete a BEd in Australia. He worked as a teacher in several South African schools before becoming the Deputy Principal at Ixopo High, a small town boarding school.

CHAPTER 6

Interracial Friendships: Sacrificial Blacks, "Reformed" Whites

Fictional interracial friendships typically depict Africans as either a "lost race" to be sacrificed or as post-Apartheid schoolmates to facilitate White redemption. Implicit in the first category is the social Darwinian notion that populations are either "fit" or "unfit" for survival in the developing world. Lesley Beake's *A Cageful of Butterflies* (1989) juxtaposes a White farm family (the survivors) and a Black "homeland" community (depicted as essentially obsolete in modern times).

In the second category (the post-election novels), White teenagers shed their white supremacist beliefs with the help of various mentors. In Elana Bregin's *The Red-Haired Khumalo* (1994), the protagonist's Black stepfather wins her over, but since the author uses him as a mouthpiece for White viewpoints, a reconstructed "New South Africa" barely surfaces. In Dennis Bailey's *Kletho* (1994), an array of Black and White high school students are integrated prior to the 1994 democratic elections. Although a White child must unlearn his prejudices, this child is not presented as a serious problem. The "problem" children in the school are primarily Blacks, teenagers who are con artists, manipulators, sex offenders, and people who capitalize on White guilt. With this set of Black/White distinctions established by the novelists (i.e., Whites striving to atone and Blacks striving to take unfair advantage), the wisdom of the whole post-Apartheid desegregation policy is called into question.

A CAGEFUL OF BUTTERFLIES

This novel sets forth a tragedy—a Black child dies while rescuing a

White child—and on the surface it is a moving account of loyalty and self-sacrifice. However, the details point to an antiquated or dysfunctional Black community, a group that is either dying out or existing only as exploited farm workers who love their servitude. These Africans seem to exist outside history, since they are totally unconnected with the liberationist Black farm movement that is struggling for justice. As the plot unfolds, there are no Blacks working for social change; there are only those headed for extinction and those reveling in a life of self-immolation.

At the outset, an African/European friendship is introduced. The White protagonist's mother describes her Zulu servant: "Maina was more than an employee. She was my friend" (12). But this friendliness had no meaningful connection to the survival of Maina's community. Maina herself dies, her husband has already died as the result of breathing coal dust, and the African community has no viable future. Maina' father, Mubi, believes there is no recourse but to give Maina's deaf-mute son (Mponyane) to the White family that had once employed his daughter. He says, "[T]here is no one else" (1). At the end, young Mponyane will die also, and before his death he looks at his village and describes its inability to help him:

> There was nothing for him there. He saw a sudden clear picture of the place and the people who live there. They were only the people who weren't living somewhere else. The left-overs. (90)

Why does this boy call his African family and friends "left-overs"? Why is the place they inhabit so meaningless? Why has the young boy been given away, and his mother before him? Is all this dislocation just an act of nature, or has the Apartheid regime played a part? There is no hint of governmental complicity. An ongoing colonized status appears in the story as an unalterable "given"—as what "nature" intended.

It is true that Mponyane's grandfather feels compassion for the Saunderson farm family. The son, Frank, is sickly, the father is imprisoned for an alleged embezzelment at the coal mine, and the mother can scarcely pay the bills. But this novel is more than a tale of mutual Black/White helpfulness. It places a White community in contrast to an indigenous African community, and a White over Black hierarchy is assumed. A Black duty to serve is assumed. A displacement from one's ancestral lands is assumed. Authority, domination, ownership—these seem to belong to the White community as a natural right, whereas African villagers have complacently surrendered their lands and their autonomy. At the end, even a young life is willingly surrendered.

Hardships endured by the farm wife are central to the book's call for sympathy. She copes with a crop-destroying drought, a son who is too weak to fend off bullies, and a crisis in morale as the townsfolk ostracize her and insist upon her husband's guilt. Conditions for Black families are treated differently. It is not seen as problematic that Black men work the mines, that Black women tend the crops on White farms, that only the very old are left in the deserted Kraals to raise young Zulu children. Why are the Zulu women not working for their own families and economies? Why must the Zulu men be separated from their wives and children? Why are African children not blessed with schooling and medical treatment? Why is the coal mine physician the only one to supply a diagnosis of Mponyane's condition and prospects? Why is company charity the boy's only hope for gaining admittance to a school for the deaf? In any case, the charity is denied on the grounds that a swarm of charity-seekers would descend upon White-owned businesses.

Apartheid policies are not connected with any of the foregoing questions. Instead, the company manager is simply a hardhearted fellow (and in the end we learn that he committed the theft attributed to Mr. Saunderson). If there is a political system driving Blacks to total dependency, that system never surfaces. Instead the farm workers are portrayed as contented peons in an idyllic setting:

> It was quiet on the farm. There was a rhythm to the days that brought a certain comfort. Early in the morning old Induna would bang an iron pipe against a bit of railway track that hung from the pepper tree, and a chattering flock of Zulu women would descend on the farmyard, smiling and laughing with each other. Induna would solemnly allocate their tasks for the day. . . . Induna himself did no real work. He was too old. Instead he dozed beside the hut where the tools were kept and maintained a dignified appearance for any visitors who might come. (29)

This bucolic picture is totally at odds with the actual conditions of Black farm laborers. In the 1960s the government set up special "Bantu" Labour Boards with jurisdiction over all farm laborers, labor tenants, and squatters (Magubane 1990, 144). Using these Boards to implement new rules, the government phased out labor tenants and squatters on White farms. African farm laborers (about half a million) had to register as full-time "farm labor" or else face eviction. This was a no-win proposition. If one registered as a farm laborer, this required separation from all unemployed family members (these members were forced to migrate to a bantustand). It also meant a wage at the lower end of the usual scale of 12–18 rands per month. If the workers refused this arrangement, they faced eviction and the loss of the value of their property and livestock, since White farmers refused to compensate them at market prices (145).

Laborers on a farm like the Saunderson's would have been subject to strict pass regulations, and typically such workers lived in derelict housing and subsisted on meager rations. Family members left in the kraal faced excruciating poverty: malnutrition, disease, unhealthy sanitation, and a lack of health and education services. This neglect was part of Apartheid's rationale for "homelands." The bantustands were set aside as "catchment areas for blacks who [could] not find work in 'white South Africa.'" (Leach 1987, 85).

As Beake's story of the Saunderson family winds down, the deaf child's inability to communicate with people causes him more and more mental stress, and by the time Mponyane dies, it almost seems like a case of merciful, divine intervention. As a mudslide engulfs Mponyane, he catches hold of Frank and tosses him to a rock outcrop where his friend will be safe. The reader is told that now the dead African boy will no longer suffer the "cageful of butterflies" in his head—the swarm of ideas he could never share with others. The novel ends with poetic words that are supposedly comforting: "Over the soft grass, a cloud of yellow butterflies danced; and were free" (99). This is "freedom" only in Apartheid terms. It is a propaganda ploy that makes Africans seem utterly expendable and conveniently self-immolating.

Such a story line allows neither place nor space for dynamic African communities. White characters are positioned as the inheritors of African land and the rulers of every public and personal condition. The novelist refers explicitly to Mponyane's nobility, but the boy's benevolence is seen only within the imperialist tradition that creates token Black saints, and then manipulates them to enhance the prospects of White characters.

Book reviewers in Britain and South Africa did not see this novel in relation to the imperialism we have described above. The book was awarded two South African book prizes: the FitzPatrick Award in 1990 and the M-Net Prize (English section) in 1991. It was warmly applauded by Dorothy Atkinson (1996) in the *School Librarian* (a British journal). Atkinson sees Beake as a writer who "conveys simply and vividly the beauty of her country as well as its problems." As a novelist, says Atkinson, Beake writes "in such a way that middle school children will . . . enjoy the story while beginning to find the problems interesting" (29). This assessment ignores the White-over-Black treatment of characterization. It ignores the distortion of farm labor realities. It suggests that children will have a good learning experience. Our view is that what is learned here will have to be unlearned.

In South Africa, Jay Heale (1996) praised the novel in these terms: "It's polished, clever writing; bitter-tasting and blunt in style, and varied in its storytelling point of view" (36). We think the "bitter taste" is present, but no one in this novel is bitter about the way Africans are subjugated or expendable. On the contrary, a Black child's death is described in upbeat, inspirational language. No one is bitter about the denial of health care and schooling for this young African. Beake apparently takes government-induced injustices for granted, and this perspective reaches into the sphere of book criticism as well.

POST-ELECTION FRIENDSHIP: *THE RED-HAIRED KHUMALO*

When Elana Bregin creates Chelsea Forster, she connects her young protagonist with the "change of heart" formula that has a long history in children's literature. When Chelsea changes her name to Chelsea Khumalo (the surname of her Black stepfather), we are to believe that Chelsea is changing her inner self, that a truly post-Apartheid era has arrived. But in our view, Chelsea does not achieve a convincing reformation because the author's perspective is not anti-Apartheid.

To Bregin's credit, she does show Chelsea challenging her own inaccurate definition of racism and discovering its flaws. But this improvement occurs alongside Bregin's interpretation of recent South African history, in which history follows the conventional Apartheid line. She makes her analysis look plausible by inventing a Black character (the stepfather) to use as her mouthpiece. This stand-in for Bregin (Chester Khumalo) embodies a blame-the-victim interpretation of recent South African history.

After Chelsea's mother marries this Black college librarian, Chelsea must share her home not only with the Black stepfather, but also with his teenaged son, Nkululeko. This development is so embarrassing that she initially conceals the existence of her new family. But in time she concludes that having an aversion to people constitutes a form of racism, and she will hate herself if she persists in that mode of thinking. However, the author's stereotyping of the Black teenager as loud-mouthed, arrogant, inconsiderate, and sexist will make many readers feel alienated, even as Chelsea is tempering her own alienation and hostility. When Nkululeko is assaulted by the police in a case of mistaken identity, this does not entirely override the negative portrait that has already been drawn.

At best, Chelsea (and the reader) moves only in the direction of greater tolerance for obnoxious people. Chelsea can be sympathetic when such a person is treated cruelly, but a friendship that is one of true mutuality can never develop. On the one hand, the girl unlearns racism, but the boy is not transformed. He remains outside the norms of good behavior: outside the domain of polite manners (he disrupts a meeting of Chelsea's debating club), outside healthy hygienic practice (he uses her towels, hairbrush, and as Chelsea suspects, her toothbrush), outside the rules of household fairness (he leaves the dinner clean-up to Chelsea).

When a degree of mutual consideration does begin to emerge, this is because Chester (the stepfather) intervenes. He explains to Chelsea how much Nkululeko has suffered. This tête-à-tête between stepfather and stepdaughter opens the way for Bregin's editorial statements about South Africa's troubles. First there is a spread-the-guilt motif. Chester reassures Chelsea that "we are all a bit guilty [of being racist]" (67). The plot is contrived here to prove that Nkululeko is a racist, so Chelsea need not worry about her attitudes. Nkululeko has objected to his father's marriage to a White woman, and has told his stepsister that "two different species [cannot mate]" (66). Now Chelsea feels off the hook since her Black counterpart verbalizes her own racist creed.

Next Chester asserts that there was an equality in the cruel, racist behavior of Blacks and Whites during the anti-Apartheid school boycotts. That is, on the one hand White police "burst into their classrooms" and beat up teachers. On the other hand, Black organizers tortured and killed nonconforming students by placing burning tires around their bodies (i.e., they "necklaced" them) (67). This tit for tat explanation makes Apartheid's war *against* Black people appear as legitimate as the *anti*-Apartheid war to achieve Black liberation. This is an Apartheid-driven analysis. (Moreover, this explanation about equal Black/White guilt is not very equal—i.e., White police beat up people; Black dissidents murder and torture them.)

Finally, there is a lecture about how Blacks should feel no bitterness. Chester explains that his eldest son was killed by the police while in detention, and this has made Nkululeko bitter. According to Bregin's scenario, Chester sees no reasonableness in this emotion in his one surviving son. Nkululeko, he says, had simply become "obsessed with 'the struggle'" and at the age of thirteen had "wildly" threatened to escape to Zambia and join the people's army (67–68). Why is it an "obsession" to join in the fight against those who murder your brother? If Nkululeko's reaction to a slain sibling was "wild," what was the father's reaction? Apparently it was nothing to speak of. In fact, Chelsea exclaims that what she admired in this discussion with her stepfather was the fact that there was "no bitterness in his manner, no self-pity for the hardships he had suffered" (68).

What does this editorial by a Black spokesperson say about a "New South Africa"? Bregin's plan for the transition seems to be two-fold: (1) blame the horrors of Apartheid on Blacks and Whites equally, and (2) urge Blacks to feel no self-pity or bitterness about the murder of their children—murder that was officially sanctioned and discharged. We would argue that these are intolerable ground rules for friendship and reconciliation. They miscarry justice. They evade history. If a writer recycles stereotypes, blames victims, applauds the suppression of legitimate feelings, and does all this in the name of interracial camaraderie, there is reason for critical skepticism. Such a "unity" program is at best wrong-headed.

But a South African prize jury and a prominent American children's literature journal—VOYA (*Voices of Youth Advocates*)— had only praise for this work. The Sanlam Gold Prize for Youth Literature was bestowed on *The Red-Haired Khumalo*, and in the United States, Carol Littlejohn celebrated this novel in her overview of South African fiction. Littlejohn (1996) sees the White protagonist (Chelsea) and the Black protagonist (Nkululeko) as twin culprits prior to their gradual anti-racist education. She likes the even-handedness of presenting indigenous Africans and colonizing Whites as equal contributors to South African problems. Morover, "Bregin tackles all the emotions and problems in a believable and satisfying plot, something I have not encountered in other recommended young adult books on this topic" (200).

Dennis Bailey's *Kletho* receives a similarly glowing report from

Littlejohn in her discussion of recent South African titles. Like Bregin, Bailey has a gift, says Littlejohn, for "blend[ing] interracial relationships in believable yet exciting plots" (200). Like Bregin, Bailey also highlights a racism-to-nonracism conversion.

KLETHO

Mark is the first character in this story to undergo conversion—a gradual move away from racist attitudes. Kletho is the "garden boy" from the "Old South Africa" period, the son of the housekeeper. Mark's dad is a clergyman, and since the Reverend has repented also, he is urging Kletho to move in with the family. This will facilitate his son's redemption, or so he believes. Mark, however, is placed by the author on high moral ground because he will not let anyone push him around or try to "legislate" his social life. Mark's conversion comes through direct experiences with Kletho. (The best of which is being rescued by Kletho from drowning!)

The "liberal" parents are seen by their son as quite pushy (giving him a Zulu middle name, for example), and this makes Mark somewhat rebellious. Black characters in this tale are serious offenders; they are virtual experts at intimidation and deception. Perhaps they learned this behavior from the ANC, which is never referred to except as an organization that intimidates people. For example, Mark observes ANC campaign strategies as he travels into the neighboring township: "Pro-ANC graffiti plastered the corrugated iron walls of a bus-shelter, warning any with alternative viewpoints to keep silent" (21).

Such strong-arm tactics are accompanied by more subtle forms of intimidation. In an episode in which Kletho's cousin molests Mark's girlfriend, Mark explains to the young woman that *she* "will be found culpable." "They're black, Rose," says Mark. "Their story is very believable . . . Their cultural naivety will be weighed against your irresponsible behavior" (30). (Rose, who is fond of dancing, had joined three African youths to learn African dances.) Blackness is used here, as in other scenes, as an expedient way for Africans to manipulate people and events.

At the climax, Kletho's cousin and the son of a police officer are forced to share a cabin during a camping trip, thereby discovering each other's shared humanity. Kletho and Mark also share an experience: they have both been sexually molested by a male teacher. And so it goes in this novel. Various pairs are created to reveal the potential camaraderie of Black and White students, but the Blacks are stereotypically portrayed. They are cunning (as when tricking Rose), licentious ("No amount of stress could divert Thulani's obsession with women"), and drunken (Kletho's brother is killed when riding with a drunk driver and his mourners promptly indulge themselves with "highly intoxicating African beer"). They are also politically counterproductive (a defaced township wall carries the sign: "Say no to elections—the government always wins") (21).

All these scenes add up to a group portrait of a township—a portrait in which the values ascribed to Africans are not the ones Whites commonly call "common virtues." Thus the friendships seem tenuous at best, resting on no solid foundation of mutuality.

* *

When an author contrives an African population and then introduces the longstanding, negative clichés about Africans, how can the story evoke a post-Apartheid environment? How can the use of a smart-mouthed young narrator (as in *Kletho*) cover over a white supremacist bias? Is a New South Africa presented in the light of African history, experience, and philosophy? And what needs to be said about the promotion of *The Red-Haired Khumalo* and *Kletho* in the American journal *VOYA*?

The American and South African literary worlds are not that far apart.[1] Anthony W. Marx (1998) compared the two nations at the end of the twentieth century and found similar racial divisions. In fact, he saw "divergent racial orders" being shaped in the U.S. and South Africa by some of the same political and economic forces (1). In the same vein, D. S. Massey and N. A. Denton in *American Apartheid* (1993) make the assertion that "although America's apartheid may not be rooted in the legal strictures of its South African relative, it is no less effective in perpetuating racial inequality . . ." (quoted in Schutte 1995, 336). For our purposes, we have focused on the way literature is able to create a "symbolic repertoire" supporting race discrimination. That repertoire is traceable in fictional works and similarly apparent in works of literary criticism (the additional means for legitimizing the repertoire). Both professional establishments are culpable when they misstate the grounds for interracial amicability.

Among the greatest of human inventions is a binding friendship, but what are its demands? A Buganda proverb issues this warning:

Some people are like cowdung. It looks dry but the inside is slippery.

An Egyptian proverb posits a high standard:

The image of friendship is truthfulness. (Knappert 1989, 51)

WORKS CITED

Atkinson, Dorothy. 1996. Review of Lesley Beake's *A Cageful of Butterflies.* *School Librarian* 44: 29.

Bailey, Dennis. 1994. *Kletho.* Isando: Heinemann Publishers.

Beake, Lesley. [1989] 1995. *A Cageful of Butterflies.* Cape Town: Maskew Miller Longman. Reprint, London: Bodley Head/Red Fox.

Bregin, Elana. 1994. *The Red-Haired Khumalo.* Cape Town: Maskew Miller Longman.

Fredrickson, George M. 1981. *White Supremacy: A Comparative Study in American and South African History.* New York and Oxford: Oxford University Press.

Heale, Jay. 1996. Review of Lesley Beake's *A Cageful of Butterflies.* In *From the Bushveld to Biko: The Growth of South African Children's Literature in English from 1907 to 1992 Traced through 110 Notable Books,* ed. Jay Heale, 36. Grabouw, S.A.: Bookchat.

Knappert, Jan. 1989. *The A–Z of African Proverbs.* London: Karnak House.

Leach, Graham. 1987. *South Africa: No Easy Path to Peace.* Rev. ed. London: Methuen.

Littlejohn, Carol. 1996. Review of Elana Bregin's *The Red-Haired Khumalo.* In "Journey to J'burg: My Travels in South African Young Adult Literature." *VOYA* (*Voices of Youth Advocates*): 200.

Magubane, Bernard Makhosezwe. [1979] 1990. *The Political Economy of Race and Class in South Africa.* Reprint, New York and London: Monthly Review Press.

Marx, Anthony W. 1998. *Making Race and Nation: A Comparison of South Africa, the United States, and Brazil.* Cambridge: Cambridge University Press.

Schutte, Gerhard. 1995. *What Racists Believe: Race Relations in South Africa and the United States.* Thousand Oaks, CA, London, and New Delhi: Sage Publications.

NOTE

1. There is a long history of parallel political, economic, and cultural conditions in the United States and South Africa. See George M. Fredrickson's seminal study, *White Supremacy: A Comparative Study in American and South African History* (1981).

CHAPTER 7

Interracial Romance: "Scientific" Racism Persists

At one level of consciousness, authors such as Toeckey Jones[1] (*Skindeep*, 1986) and Lawrence Bransby (*Down Street*, 1989) seem to understand the irrationality and cruelty of the white supremacy myth. But their rejection of this myth does not translate into novels that avoid the stereotyping of Blacks. Instead, Africans are associated with Communist "terrorists" or township criminals, and the myth receives implicit support. Interrelationships that could serve as a denial of Apartheid's dehumanizing tenets fail to emerge.

Such ambivalence about racism is particularly noticeable in novels featuring interracial romance. Interracial coupling was made illegal by the Prohibition of Mixed Marriages Act in 1949 and by the prohibition of all interracial sexual activity in the Immorality Act of 1950. *Skindeep* deals directly with these laws and their repeal in the 1980s, yet the novel seems imbued with the pseudo-science upon which these laws were based. Lawmakers invoked this "science" in defense of the anti-marriage law: "[It is] scientific to hold yourself aloof from a race with a lower civilization and . . . more limited intellectual powers . . ." (quoted in Dubow 1995, 182). Apartheid became more consolidated as lawmakers played upon fears of miscegenation and scientists proclaimed the dangers of "tainted blood," "race degeneration," and other spurious risks. *Skindeep* questions this "science" on the one hand, but on the other hand it separates the lovers in the end and undercuts its earlier liberationist theme. More important, nearly all the Black characters except the "Coloured" protagonist display what the lawmakers' claims warned of: "limited intellectual powers." Even the hero emerges finally as one of the despised "ethnical types," as a Black nationalist.

SKINDEEP

Toeckey Jones exposes the evil of color prejudice, but then abandons that theme and its progressive implications. He makes the "Coloured" hero so racist that he will not accept positive change—in this case, the overturning of the miscegenation prohibition. The protagonist, Dave, will not adapt to the new rules and marry his White fiancee, Rhonda. Additionally, Blacks are treated as superstitious, primitive, and out of tune with the modern world. They are sometimes enamoured by whiteness, or so opposed to it that separatism is adopted as the solution to Apartheid's injustices. The novel says, in essence, that if Blacks have their way, White-initiated Apartheid will be replaced with Black-initiated Apartheid. So why not just support the status quo?

The plot line moves Dave around in two officially separate racial worlds. He is given away by his "Coloured" mother to a Jewish family that employs his mother as a servant. At that point, all contact between mother and son is terminated. We learn nothing of the "Coloured" mother except that she has always viewed Dave as her best child and has openly referred to him in these terms. This favoritism stems from the light hue of Dave's skin and from the practical advantages that a White identity will include. Even in infancy, Dave's hair is meticulously straightened to give an impression of Caucasian heritage. This maternal partisanship causes jealousy in the other offspring and nourishes a sense of self-hate in them.

Only one of Dave's siblings is lifted out of this false consciousness, and this progressive step only seals his doom. He has become a promoter of Black nationalism, and the novelist makes a point of depicting Black nationalism and Black consciousness as futile and misguided. Thus when Dave's brother loses his life at the hands of the police, this tragedy is presented as an essentially self-inflicted event. We are told that the young man's hatred of Whites is his sole motivation for political activism, and this attitude can only prove destructive to life and the creation of a viable democracy. In the end, therefore, the killing of this young person appears legitimate. The reader has been given no understanding of anti-Apartheid street demonstrations and no sympathy for Black leaders, so the young man's death is skimmed over as something unimportant. In fact, the book's readers may well think that he got what he deserved.

Dave's mother has also had a tragic life since her separation from her light-complexioned child. When Dave accidentally finds her, she is a crippled street beggar, and this encounter between mother and son causes Dave to disclose to Rhonda who he really is. Rhonda instantly becomes "violently sick" (198). As she is vomiting and collapsing into total panic, she is remembering that a Black child may be occupying her womb. According to the white supremacy myth, race is determined biologically, and biology has denied full humanness to Africans. This explains Dave's efforts to pass for White and his bitterness when his masquerade is exposed.

The novel makes a pointed contrast between this embittered, unforgiving young man and his miraculously reformed girlfriend. Rhonda has read a stack of banned books and emerged as a new woman for a New South Africa. The years of indoctrination have been swept away in a moment. But Dave is another number entirely. He will not be reconciled. He will not emulate the good White teenagers—Rhonda and her friends—who are all moving forward in reconstructing South Africa and finding a good life. Even Rhonda's most hedonistic, drug-addicted classmates have regenerated themselves, gone off to art school, or joined the anti-Apartheid movement.

Turning to the other Black characters in *Skindeep*, we find the conventional, stereotypic portraits. Sophie, for example, is a faithful servant in Rhonda's household. She is a clownish figure, a religious fanatic who is "unstoppable" in invoking the name of Jesus (89). She clearly has no capacity to grasp anything as abstract as religious thought, despite her babbling about Biblical heroes, and when Rhonda takes a trip by air, Sophie says she is like Jonah entering the belly of the fish. When she sees Dave's bald head, she turns him into the Old Testament Samson. Sophie is not a danger to the household, being too languorous and apolitical to go on the attack, but her husband, we are told, just might be a threat. He is a potential cutthroat because the Communists are allegedly recruiting Blacks, and the whole servant class has become furtive, morose, and menacing. The servants no longer reveal, says the novelist, what they are privately thinking (24).

Generally speaking, Sophie comes off as the proverbial minstrel comic. There is no background information about her real life: her forced separation from her husband as the result of a live-in job, her low wage scale, her offspring or lack of offspring, her friendships. She is a robot who quotes Scripture. She has no sense of self, and the reader has no opportunity to know her except as a ridiculous accessory. All we see is someone devoid of credible human qualities.

If South Africa was indeed evolving in a positive direction in 1986 (as suggested in this book's focus on miscegenation), what is to be the future for Sophie? It is unlikely that the reader will care enough to ask. Even if Dave and Rhonda had married in the end, their offspring could have ended up in the same labor pool as Sophie, and received as little economic and social justice. With Jones's implicit acceptance of unfair labor laws, a servant such as Sophie needs to come across as undeserving of anything better, and this is what the stereotype accomplishes.

So the question remains: Why does the novelist introduce miscegenation laws, show the repeal of those laws, and then suggest that such action is pointless? Why does he insist that Blacks are not progressive enough to change? Why does perpetual separateness (Apartheid) end up as a Black, and not a White, creation? This turns history on its head, but Western book reviewers did not object. *Skindeep* was praised by a New Jersey high school librarian as "an interesting, readable book" (Smith 1987, 31). The overall rating is "Recommended." *Horn Book* magazine was even more effusive:

> The dialogue, smouldering sexuality, and emotions of adolescents are beautifully captured—as is the intensely tragic landscape against which they act. Consequently, the South African novelist has created a novel which cannot help but make young readers reflect on the nature of racial prejudice and its implications for all nations. (Silvey 1987, 216)

Additionally, the book reviewer comments that the plea to be judged on one's merits "makes this book universal rather than particular in its concerns" (216). In Philadelphia a reviewer liked "the sensitive prose about issues of interest to adolescents" (Edwards 1987, 31). None of these respondents say anything about the untenable White-over-Black presumptions. This race hierarchy remains as Dave and Rhonda part company, since the now redeemed Rhonda is placed on the higher moral ground.

In a book about law and literature, John Morrison (1996) notes that the subtexts of a children's book are significant: "As we examine children's books we should be aware of . . . the coded grammars . . . that are contained there beneath the surface" (133). Hierarchy, he adds, is a "value" unmistakably "communicated within this genre" (134).

This observation is borne out in the Jones novel and in Lawrence Bransby's *Down Street*. In the latter, Blacks are a threat to your very life if you are White; "Coloureds" will thrash any Whites they can catch. But the story's White schoolboy hero just wants to be romantic.

DOWN STREET

As in *Skindeep*, there is no reconciliation between Whites and "Coloureds" in *Down Street*. The "Coloured" community is unable to rise above its benighted race consciousness. The White protagonist, Ted, explains to the reader how racist Christina, his "Coloured" girl-friend, is:

> I noticed she used the word "we" and "us" not to refer to her fami-ly, but to coloureds. Even in her general conversation she differenti-ated between whites and coloureds as if the separation, the different-ness, was complete; like two different forms of life. (71)

Ted wonders why he must forever defend his identity: "Practically everything we spoke about came back to it [color]. I wondered if we would *ever* be able to get away from it" (76). Poor Ted. He searches for "a way to confront her with [his] existence" (97). Given all this White anguish, one would never guess that a White government has made mixed-race romance illegal.

The central fact of Apartheid—the denial of Black/White equality—is threaded throughout this narrative as Blacks are made the mouth-piece of this non-egalitarian philosophy. Christina's mother speaks the pro-Apartheid line when she says to Ted: "You let [Christina] find a coloured boy to go out with—one of her own kind" (95). Christina's father tells Ted that the relationship must "end now, today," because "you are taking on the entire country . . . and it *cannot* be" (91). The "Coloureds" are depicted as acquiescing to Apartheid, and the noble White teenager must also reluctantly acquiesce: "[Deep down] I knew he was right. We had been living in a make-believe world" (91). The way these scenes are set up, we have "Coloureds" in the pro-Apartheid frontlines, and Whites sadly follow. As in *Skindeep*, White-instigated Apartheid would simply be followed by Black-instigated Apartheid if the opportunity presented itself. Ted explains this to Christina as the human condition: if the present adult generation disappeared, the kids would probably grow up and "the various shades would gang togeth-er and try to make sure they were not on the bottom rung of the lad-der" (67).

Not only would the "various shades gang together," but the "shades" are arranged with Blacks at the bottom, "Coloureds" in the middle, and Whites on top. This spectrum comes into the foreground when Ted fears for his safety. He notes that Blacks and "Coloureds" will undoubtedly "take out their frustrations" on someone:

> I mean, black gangs were grabbing people they didn't like and burning them, setting them on fire with a petrol-filled car tyre forced over their shoulders. . . . [T]he coloureds have never done that, only blacks. A few stabbings, though. (77)

When the "Coloureds" catch up with Ted, they beat him up badly before a sympathetic Indian arrives to give him a lift. The Indian warns him that the "Coloureds" have knives and "They always drunk, those guys" (101).

The field of science has been used in Apartheid circles to explain these human categories. A 1955 government report alluded to distinctive groups as "organisms" with distinctive "development." According to historian Leonard Thompson (1985), the report "relied on racial theory in an extreme organicist form, likening races to organisms that have distinctive cultural as well as physical properties and characteristic courses of development" (197). In particular, the report stressed Black/White differences ("Europeans and Bantu . . . are culturally and racially alien to each other") and did not mince words about the alleged superiority of Europeans: the "European national organism [had] a form of Western Civilization as its vital basis." This was a "higher cultural content" than the content of Bantu culture (197–198).

Hierarchies in the Bransby novel echo such pseudo-scientific beliefs. We hear a brief comment about Ted's degraded homelife, but what reaches the reader at close range is African degradation. Besides the murderous street gangs, we encounter Christina's devious, flirtatious sister; her churlish, tyranical mother; and her politically appeasing father and grandfather. Grandfather preaches about Jesus, and Christina explains to Ted how "we would be together again one day" because of "Jesus and Heaven" (73). As in so many pro-Apartheid narratives, *Down Street* joins heavenly peace with social separateness.

This idea is reinforced when a Black social worker lectures at Ted's school. She says that four years in England have taught her self-worth, and she is therefore able to "laugh at petty racism and put it behind her . . ." (41). She had encountered racist remarks in England (e.g., "What a pity she's black"), but she had "laughed at this—not bitterly, but openly and with obvious enjoyment" (41). Is the novelist gently preparing readers to accept Christina's disappointments? They will see her lose her job, lose her boyfriend, submit to the appeasement policy of her parents, and end up with a hopeless, threat-filled life. Is she to laugh at this? Avoid bitterness? Treat racist slurs "with obvious enjoyment"?

South African book critics have seen no problem with all this. English professor Elwyn Jenkins (1993) recommends the novel effusively: "*Down Street* is the best—and also the most devastating— South African youth novel on this theme [schoolboys examining racism] that I have read" (143). In his book *South African Authors and Illustrators*, Jay Heale (1994) says that Bransby "was given suitable recognition when *Down Street* received the M.E.R. prize from Nasionale Boekhandel in 1989" (8).

The critics, like the novelist, seem to see Apartheid as a "given" and people of color as raising no strong objections. Admittedly, Bransby does let his hero evolve. He takes Ted from the point where his "flesh creeps" (56) to the point where he can touch Christina's hand without flinching. But the novel predominantly contradicts this change of heart and implies that separation of races is an "absolute" that "Coloureds" endorse.

* *

Race determinism evolved in South Africa as one way to rationalize the concept of "nation," and specifically the privileges of a White "nation." The meaning of Apartheid was symbolized most powerfully in the Prohibition of Mixed Marriages Act, the law that ensured no loss of "nation" as the white supremacist purists perceived it. By constructing stories that debate this issue and then come down on the side of race separation, Jones and Bransby connect with the "scientific" race theory that government officials used to bolster their "race purity" program. As one official concluded: "Marriage is only complete when it is a synthesis of biological, eugenic, sociological, ethical and religious ideals" (quoted in Dubow 1995, 182). When Saul Dubow notes how novels carried the race purity message—how they "provide a particularly rich source for . . . images which underscore notions of [Black] moral and physical degeneration"—he could have looked to children's novels to persuasively validate his point (187).

WORKS CITED

Bransby, Lawrence. 1989. *Down Street*. Cape Town: Tafelberg.

Dubow, Saul. 1995. *Scientific Racism in Modern South Africa*. Cambridge: Cambridge University Press.

Edwards, Beverly. 1987. Review of *Skindeep*. *Best Sellers* 46, 10: 406.

Heale, Jay. 1994. *South African Authors and Illustrators*. Grabouw, S.A.: Bookchat.

Jenkins, Elwyn. 1993. *Children of the Sun: Selected Writers and Themes in South African Children's Literature*. Johannesburg: Ravan Press.

Jones, Toeckey. 1986. *Skindeep*. New York: Harper.

Morrison, John and Christine Bell, eds. 1996. *Tall Stories: Reading Law and Literature*. Aldershot, England, Brookfield, USA, Sydney, and Singapore: Dartmouth Publishing Company Ltd.

Silvey, Anita. 1987. Review of *Skin Deep*. *Horn Book* 63, 2: 216.

Smith, Mary. 1987. Review of *Skin Deep*. *The Book Report* 5, 5: 31.

Thompson, Leonard. 1985. *The Political Mythology of Apartheid*. New Haven and London: Yale University Press.

NOTE

1. Toeckey Jones was born in South Africa and moved in 1971 to London, where he works as a full-time writer. His first children's novel was *Go Well, Stay Well* (1980). *Skindeep* is his second novel geared for young adult readers.

CHAPTER 8

Stories of the Supernatural: Misreading African Tradition

African folklore is sometimes used as a vehicle for suggesting Black/White unity within a South African context. This intention falls short of success when the lore becomes a pastiche of "heart of darkness" stereotypes. Such is the case in Carolyn Parker's *Witch Woman on the Hogsback* (1987) and Marguerite Poland's *The Shadow of the Wild Hare* (1986). Black characters are mired in a dysfunctional, pre-modern world and White characters briefly enter that domain as benefactors, but the European notion of carrying a "White man's burden" can hardly produce a lasting basis for friendship. Instead, this White-over-Black perspective adheres firmly to the oppressive Apartheid agenda. The African protagonists in both the Parker and Poland stories represent a pre-conceived primitivism—a backwardness that fits them for servitude and little else in today's world.

Although these writers use mythology in ways that underscore an alleged primitive mindset, they also appear respectful toward Africa. But young, Western readers generally lack accurate information to draw upon as they sort out this ambivalence and try to understand where these authors are coming from and where they are taking them. An African readership, however, can easily understand the misreading of tradition that these narratives incorporate and reinforce.

THE WITCH WOMAN ON THE HOGSBACK

The Witch Woman on the Hogsback is a story about "good" and "evil," "strength" and "weakness," Black Africans and White

Caucasians. It is a story about domination and preservation, about the "known" and the "unknown," about might and right. This content raises certain questions: Is the novel, first and last, a story of the supernatural? Is it about White domination and Black survival? Is it about educating Whites to unwittingly think along colonialist lines? There is nothing wrong with adapting a myth, proverb, or legend into a novellength story. There is nothing wrong when outsiders try to write about a culture and a people's tradition about which they are interested. But a serious problem arises when the storyteller is Eurocentrically biased, or when the teller has scanty background information and unknowingly misrepresents a people's cultural traditions.

The protagonists in *Witch Woman* are two thirteen-year-olds: Luvuyo (an African) and Kate (a Caucasian whose mother is unconscious as the result of a car accident). This pair became acquainted two years earlier when Kate visited her aunt and uncle, the employers of Luvuyo's mother. In this new encounter there are extraordinary circumstances that set the stage for a potential bonding of Black and White. These new conditions include a cast of supernatural beings and a wildly phantasmagoric plot to overthrow the benign forces of nature. The opening page alludes to Kate, who is inexplicably the target of much supernatural malice:

> The witch woman crouched over the embers of a fire. Its light flickered on uneven walls of rock and streaks of snow on the stone-strewn earth. From the folds of her cloak, she drew a piece of woven cloth. She laid it on the glowing coals, muttering softly, then leaned forward to study it as it twisted and flared in the heat. In the moving threads, she saw the delicate shape of a child with yellow hair. She drew her breath sharply as if in anger or fear. At a touch of her finger, the pattern changed and she saw the child bowed in anguish and pain, and the shadow of death was cast over her. The witch smiled to herself and nodded. (1)

This fearsome White witch is migrating to Africa to do damage to the world's environment, and apparently a White South African girl is the one obstacle in her path. But the girl survives the car crash, joins her aunt and uncle at their remote rural farm, and overthrows the Witch Woman and her African consort. The plot line winds through a stream of encounters with mythical beings associated with African folklore: water sprites, warlocks, forest spirits, and others. The subtext is a series of commentaries about White superiority and White rule.

Like nearly all the South African stories we have read, the Africans here have the role of housekeepers in White homes or subsistence herders of livestock. It is not a coincidence that Luvuyo's mother is in the menial position of maid, since White superiority is central to the story as Kate sets forth to save both the environment and Luvuyo's Xhosa community. When the mythical River people are in trouble, they turn to Kate to rescue the River "Mother" from the Witch Woman: "[My little brother] weeps for our mother who has been taken from us. When he saw you, he stopped weeping and came to us saying . . . 'I have seen a white child of the land who may help us'" (17). Talala, the River Princess, gratefully tells Kate: "Bless you white child . . . your courage is great" (18).

Also reinforcing the White-over-Black hierarchy is Luvuyo's secondary status. He is only capable of leading Kate through the magical world as a preliminary guide; he must step aside as the all-powerful, fearless Kate takes over in the final showdown with the witch. And when the victory comes, Luvuyo expresses his indebtedness for learning a valuable environmentalist perspective. That is, Kate has enabled him "to hear the voices of all the People of this place" (meaning "the People of the forest and mountain, of the Earth and Air and Water") (130). Even the role of the African diviner, the igqira, is secondary to Kate's role in vanquishing evil, and the overall portrait of this religious leader is highly condescending. It calls attention to itself because it is unlikely that Parker would similarly approach a priest who professes Christianity. In fact, a Christian priest does make a brief appearance, but he remains in the background, and he is not accused of racism as is the igqira. That is, Luvuyo must warn Kate about the African community's chief diviner because he may well reject her on racist grounds: "You see, [says Luvuyo] I'm not sure whether he'll want you to see him, because you are not of my people" (30).

Luvuyo's "people" also include an aggrieved wife, Mandisa, who is so bitter about her husband's wish to "ditch" her that she turns against the entire community. She sets off to join the Witch Woman, proclaiming to the chief Elder, "I go, old man, to one who is more powerful than you and all the Amagqira [diviners] of our people" (5). There is no logical connection between this disaffected villager and the world of the witch. Rather the whole episode (including Mandisa's banishment for being in league with the devil) shows the arbitrariness with which Africans allegedly render justice. It points to pettiness and stupidity because a personal feud is allowed to overshadow everyone's welfare. Parker is setting up a community in disarray as she plots a scenario to logically bolster the cause of White intervention. She makes the intercessor, Kate, a true paragon of European tact, wisdom, and *noblesse oblige.*

The story unwinds with its overload of pretensions about integration, mutual understanding, and tolerance. If there is any Black/White unity implied in all this, it is tenuous at best, for Luvuyo will never be a part of modern South Africa. The only plot twist that gives him some status is his appointment as a diviner at the end of the tale, and this new career will not mean much (if the present igqira serves as an indicator). It will isolate him further from Kate and the modern world. It will not offer experience or occasion for action in the war against Apartheid. The ruling White minority will remain free to subjugate Luvuyo's whole community, and his mother and others like her will continue to be a servant class. His father will continue as a low-paid worker in a distant auto assembly plant. The young women and men in the Xhosa community will have no association on equal terms with the young men and women in Kate's community. In short, a social and political status quo is assured. Africans have been depicted with a hopelessly antiquated society and a one-dimensional religious system in which demons are believed to be lurking in every crevice. That, needless to say, settles the question about any equitable role for them in a modern civic community.

Parker, however, was on solid ground here in the eyes of European–South African book critics. Despite the clear-cut hierarchy of "civilized" and "uncivilized," this novel was touted as a progressive work. Jay Heale (1996) speaks of Parker's "success" in involving "modern characters with figments of African mythology." He likes the assumption of shared guilt: "the evil power," he writes approvingly, "is a mixture of European and African" (33). Writing for the international journal *Bookbird*, Andree-Jeanne Totemeyer (1992) describes the book as having "a common African cultural vision which transcends ethnic boundaries and race" (10). One wonders how this conclusion is reached, when the novelist has made the permanent separation of modern Black and White societies seem inevitable—when she implies a thousand-year gap between African and Caucasian development. This White-defined gap for Parker's protagonists means a prospect involving "different lives." The young Kate observes: "She knew that like her, he [Luvuyo] was thinking of their different lives . . ." (130). In the Apartheid context, Kate has a real future, while Luvuyo will continue in that state of passive, apolitical existence that Parker contrived for him from the outset. Kate will be gone in a flash when her mother regains consciousness. Apartheid officials will have every opportunity to maintain their exploitation of Blacks.

The cycles of juvenile book publishing are replete with unfinished socio-political myths. As in *The Witch Woman on the Hogsback*, they offer only confusion when introducing better race relations. Marguerite Poland's *The Shadow of the Wild Hare* is another case in point, a story about "the good life" lived by White children, while the African looks on and waits for crumbs.[1]

THE SHADOW OF THE WILD HARE

This novel deals more with possession (and being possessed) than with wild hares. It is about a White woman, Jacoba Pandoer, who was orphaned, shared her life with the San people, and was thereby deemed "possessed" (i.e., insane.) It is about a young White girl who has maternal instincts for wild creatures and wishes to possess a hare in order to protect it. It is about a young boy's possession of a baboon and how this kind of possession amounts to enslavement of this animal. It is about an African trapper who uses animals for bait, and when he is possessing an endangered species for this purpose, he is allegedly a menace to Africa and its environment. But another kind of possession—namely, colonization—underlies this story of Black/White relations, and this is a story that is kept well hidden.

The story line describes two sets of parents and their offspring. Willie's father fills his son with racist beliefs, and the boy gleefully spreads this malicious doctrine around the neighborhood. Rosie is the nearest neighbor and she is the novel's major protagonist. Unfortunately, her father is not much help in assuaging her racist fears. Rosie is terrified by the African trapper, Tantyi Mayekiso, who works for her father to rid his farm of marauding jackals. Her father offers little guidance to offset the barrage of white supremacist attitudes that pour in from next door. This may be in keeping with the characterization Poland has contrived, but with the exception of a brief comment from Rosie's mother ("Of course [Mayekiso] doesn't suck blood!") it leaves a thematic vacuum. There is little cultural balance or honesty finding its way to children inside or outside the book.

It is clear that Rosie is blessed with moral superiority since she seeks to liberate a wild creature (the hare). Willie, on the other hand, continues to imprison a hapless baboon. But the race relations issue is still confused because the author describes the trapper in stereotypical imagery. He is portrayed as the ultimate "primitive" and mystic, who is sneaking about with a Stone Age mentality. He provides the author with a channel for telling an African folktale, but this does not offset the images of Rosie being afraid of his "strange, dark, slanted eyes" (14). Moreover, Rosie associates this Black man with the family's Black housekeeper and is even afraid to be alone with this long-trusted servant. Throughout, Rosie is given no opportunity to know the human being who is inside the African, nor is she receiving any knowledge of her own ancestors and their appropriation of Mayekiso's ancestral lands. She is learning only the limiting traditions that separate "them" and "us," and Mayekiso has no option but to watch and wait in silence. The White landowners teach children that he is a mad monster (as Willie's father teaches Willie), or else a veritable "nothingness" in the society that prejudges Africans.

One of the most insidious misstatements has to do with the African environment, and the way Poland manipulates its history. In contrast to her theme of African culpability, people of color (whether African or Native American or any other indigenous group) did not destroy their natural habitats. In fact, one Western literary convention praised indigenes for their great *closeness* to nature. They were viewed as people who were *happily* "uncivilized"—who did not have the sciences to complicate their lives. On the downside, they lacked the sciences that would make them a "master" race in competition with other so-called races. In dealing with nature, Poland inserts a folktale about a rabbit and the moon and how the rabbit symbolizes "the words of life and death."[2] This idea is useful in a commentary on environmental abuses and alleged African obsolescence since "the Dhau [the hare in the moon] is the child of the old people and like them he is almost gone" (38). Mayekiso represents "the old [and disappearing] people," given his style of life, and he is a threat to the environmentalist. As in Parker's *The Witch Woman on the Hogsback*, Africans are seen to need Westerners to show them the conservationist path.

Besides the irony in this switch from "too natural" to "not natural enough," there is an irony in the way Jacoba Pandoer is treated skeptically and yet approvingly. Rosie depends upon Jacoba to take her to where they can release the endangered wild hare, yet the novel shows no real appreciation of the San people and their willingness to extend their families to include Jacoba, an orphaned child. In African tradition, a child belongs to the community, and this great advantage in the life of Jacoba is obscured by images of her "strangeness," her disfigured eyes, her ostracization by her neighbors. In the end, Jacoba has been a friend, but her marginalization in human society is never treated with understanding or with an awareness of the injustices stemming from her Black/White past.

Storytelling that posits the White child as the "Great White Environmentalist" (supplanting the earlier "Great White Hunter") does not, in our view, produce a great bond between Whites and Africans. But such a bond is what literary educator Elwyn Jenkins (1993) sees in this book. He comments that this novel is "elevat[ed] to a profound level of understanding, not about 'conservation', but about the relationship between South African peoples, and between them and nature" (89). He applauds Poland for her "respect for Xhosa beliefs," and for her spirituality. He says the book shows "that reconciliation of black and white must take place on a spiritual plane as well as through intellectual understanding and forgiveness of the past" (140). In contrast, we do not see the colonizing past being transcended. Blacks are presented as the people who are ignorant of vital environmental facts. Therefore to sustain the conservationist cause, these Africans *need* to be controlled. This message can hardly lead to the good "relationship between South African peoples" that Jenkins finds so compelling in Poland's effort. As for "forgiveness," this is the White theme song that has been echoing across South Africa ever since it appeared that Mandela would survive and reengage in the liberationist struggle. For Africans, the theme song is equality, mutuality, and accountability.

* *

Conservation, geology, and other aspects of natural science have a significant role, writes John M. MacKenzie (1990), "in the extension and maintenance of imperial power" (3). This extension was not just a matter of diffusing scientific information among people at the grassroots level. It constituted "a social process influenced by racial and cultural criteria" (4). Historically, conservation was an ideological matter, and the symbolic involvement of wild animals was especially important to this ideology. In a novel such as *The Shadow of the Wild Hare*, this ideology receives a new life.[3] In animal stories, there is a strong element of romanticism that appeals to conservation-minded White readers and to children. But the Black population knows that such works are often a biased White project and that "ecstatic communion" with the animal world can be a seductive cover-up for white supremacist sermons.

Another aspect of popular science in literature is the "lost world" theme. This motif gave geology a role in forming racial attitudes. Parker, in *The Witch Woman on the Hogsback*, says she was drawing upon Xhosa mythology, plus her own imagination, as she constructed Luvuyo's world, but that imagination seems embedded in colonialist tradition, as well as in the conventions of "lost world" fiction. As exotic landscapes-of-the-past were instilled in schoolbooks in the nineteenth and early twentieth centuries, so the fantasy world of Parker's imagination plays a similar part in sending a monocultural mythology to today's child readers.

Generally speaking, as the "Green Party" movement picks up more converts in Western political circles, there is more likelihood that children's literature will make continuing use of its unique natural/supernatural mix. This is a pattern dating back at least two centuries.

WORKS CITED

Heale, Jay. 1996. Review of Carolyn Parker's *Witch Woman on the Hogsback*. In *From Bushveld to Biko: The Growth of South African Children's Literature in English from 1907 to 1992 Traced through 110 Notable Books,* ed. Jay Heale, 33. Grabouw, S.A.: Bookchat.

Jenkins, Elwyn. 1993. *Children of the Sun: Selected Writers and Themes in South African Children's Literature.* Johannesburg: Ravan Press.

Parker, Carolyn. 1987. *The Witch Woman on the Hogsback.* Pretoria: De Jager-HAUM.

Poland, Marguerite. 1986. *The Shadow of the Wild Hare.* Cape Town, Johannesburg: David Philip, Publisher.

MacKenzie, John M., ed. 1990. *Imperialism and the Natural World.* Manchester and New York: Manchester University Press.

Totemeyer, Andree-Jeanne. 1992. "Impact of African Mythology on South African Juvenile Literature" (Part 2). *Bookbird* 30, 3: 10–15.

NOTES

1. Marguerite Poland grew up outside Port Elizabeth in an unspoiled natural environment, and has spent many years since in Kloof, Natal. In addition to novel-writing, she has collected and published San and Zulu folktales. In 1979 she received the first Percy FitzPatrick Award, a prize given under the auspices of the South African Institute for Librarianship and Information Science.

2. In the part of the tale recounted here, the hare is an African child that the moon turned into a hare. It drinks the water on the moon, and it changes from life to death and death to life in accordance with the phases of the moon. Rosie is told that she must not try to tame or confine this animal unless she wants to kill its spirit and thus terminate the renewals of life.

3. For further information and comment on this topic, see the authors' chapter entitled "The Lion Lobbyists: Environmentalism in an African Context," in *African Images in Juvenile Literature: Commentaries on Neocolonialist Fiction* (Jefferson, N.C., and London: McFarland & Co., 1996).

PART 3

HISTORICAL NOVELS

CHAPTER 9

The Trekking Boers: Land-Grabbing in Historical Literature

E uropean South African storytellers often use historical fiction to justify the European presence in South Africa. They rationalize the colonial enterprize with story lines that make European incursions legitimate and even inevitable. Africans are depicted as incapable of living successfully in Africa, as demonstrated by poverty and warfare. Concurrently, they are portrayed as welcoming the invaders, particularly in the way Blacks save White lives regardless of the sacrifice.

Such scenarios translate the land-grabbing of the early settlers into the right to rule Blacks on every level. In Ken Smith's *Tinde in the Mountains* (1987), Dutch, Xhosa, and San interests are shown to be mutually served by the arrival of Dutch sheepherders in the Great Fish and Seekoei River areas in the early 1800s. In Maretha Maartens's *The Black Sheep* (1989), trekboers in 1837 are presented as heroic pioneers of the Great Trek and noble conquerors of the Zulus at Blood River.

TINDE IN THE MOUNTAINS

Ken Smith's book promotes the false assumption that interactions between the Dutch and the San and Xhosa peoples were to everyone's advantage, the colonizers receiving no more than their rightful claim to the South African land base.[1] This misstates the case, as historian Leonard Thompson (1995) comments: "For the subordinated peoples, life in the colony was nasty, brutish, and short" (52). Smith positions his story at the time when the British governor of the colony had established a boundary between Dutch and Xhosa people at the Great Fish

River. This concluded the war of 1811–1812, a war to drive the Xhosa east of the river and thereby give the Dutch unchallenged control of areas they had already appropriated on the west side. To say that this meant peace between the colonizers and the colonized is a gross distorton. British military forces routed the Black farmers in the Fish River region on behalf of the Dutch farmers:

> [The colonial forces] ruthlessly expelled the Xhosa inhabitants from the land through to the Fish River, burning crops and villages and making off with thousands of head of cattle. (Thompson 1995, 55)

The Xhosa did not accept this arbitrary boundary and mounted a counterattack in 1819. But ultimately the colonial forces prevailed in creating a "neutral belt" to keep Whites and Africans apart (Thompson 1995, 74).

Despite the off-and-on conflict over land, Smith contrives a story in which the Dutch and Xhosa are closely collaborating in pushing out the San inhabitants. First the plot presents an unfolding friendship between the Dutch and Xhosa families. When young Willem (the Dutch protagonist) and young Tinde (the Xhosa protagonist) meet at the river, Willem implies that the grass is greener on Tinde's side of the border, while Tinde shares his family's opinion that the grass in greener on the Dutch side. Both boys recognize the humor in this and their friendship expands from the premise that their peoples constitute twin societies, with only the nomadic San communities causing problems.

The direction of the story line is to bring about a workable relationship among the three groups (San, Xhosa, and Dutch) and to find an improved locale for the Dutch farmers. Since the better pastoral region is San territory, the San are made to appear less able to make good use of it. In fact, they are depicted as less than fully human (they are "fierce little men" who utter "high-pitched squeals and cries") (116, 128). A hierarchy is presented, with the nomadic hunter-gatherers (the San) portrayed as irredeemably primitive and unable to save themselves. This portraiture is convenient from the European side. When new territory is coveted by the Dutch, the group that is an immediate obstacle is carefully delineated as nearing extinction—as dying out from natural causes. This implies that without European intervention, the whole clan would soon be swept into oblivion. What a contrast between this novelistic invention and the historical record—a record of wholesale slaughter and kidnapping:

> Trekboers made use of people from the indigenous hunting and gathering communities. Commandos exterminated adult hunter-gatherers but made a point of capturing children, and before they disbanded they distributed the children as well as the cattle booty among themselves. (Thompson 1995, 49)

In the novel, a San boy named Twa represents the hunter-gatherer group. He is sometimes heroic as an individual, but he carries with him the burden of an allegedly non-viable culture. His tracking skills are shown to be as acute as those of a wild creature, but this talent appears simply as a biological inheritance. Twa has lived with a Dutch family since early childhood, but his tracking skills are always intact, and they come in handy when rescuing Dutch boys who become lost in the wild. But all this changes. When Twa and the San community are suddenly shown to be lacking in self-sufficiency; they require European help. In actual fact it was "the trekboers [who] were never a self-sufficient society. They were accustomed to using coerced slave and indigenous labor" (Thompson 1995, 49).

Tinde is invited to go with Willem's family to their summer camp in the mountains. Wild game has become scarce because the herds of the sheepherding families have cropped the grass too short, leaving little for antelope herds, and since the San have traditionally lived on antelope, they are now starving. The European children persuade them to accept gifts rather than steal sheep. Guns are the key to this sudden gift-giving plan since guns can bring down the few remaining wild animals at long range. The whole area is so depleted, however, that the Dutch and the San both desire better hunting and pasturing sites. After initial doubts, the San are persuaded by the European children to continue accepting gifts in exchange for Dutch occupation of their territory.

In contrast to the San (who are too backward and happy-go-lucky for the changing economy of the region), the Xhosa are compatriots with the Boer farmers. Much of the action revolves around Willem and Tinde helping each other, but this does not translate into a relationship of true mutuality. When Tinde saves Willem from freezing to death and in the process loses his own foot from frostbite, Willem's father makes him a wooden leg and gives him a horse. The author spends pages describing the way Tinde dotes on horses, and this supposedly makes us think of this trade-off as satisfactory. Indeed, Tinde's father rhapsodizes about Dutch benevolence:

"The way these [Dutch] people from across the river care for you
amazes me. If I had not seen it with these old eyes of mine, I would
not have believed it." (109)

Actually Tinde saves Willem's life twice at the risk of his own, but
in colonialist fiction, the "lesser" beings seem to know instinctively
that they are destined to save the "superior" beings. Tinde is always
overjoyed when an opportunity presents itself. No matter that he suffers excruciating pain and loss of a limb. No matter that he incurs a
disability that limits and weakens him for a lifetime. In this story, any
connection with so-called Western civilization is worth any price.

Unfair exchanges also occur in the Dutch/San relationship. The
Dutch will receive any new farming lands that please them, while the
San will receive handouts to sustain their families. They will give up
responsibility for individual and group welfare. They will become, in
effect, hostages of the Dutch, since they can be pressured or even liq-
uidated at the prerogative of the colonizers. San acquiescence in this
arrangement is explained by showing the failure of San people to plan
for the future. The novelist, however, exaggerates this point, since in
reality, San groups did organize into loosely defined hunting areas and
acknowledged each other's specific domains.

In his "Author's Note," Smith refers to his use of colonist diaries in
developing his knowledge of his subject. He maintains that the diaries
from the early 1800s tell of "mutual dependence and amity" between
the Boer and San communities (Smith 1987, vii). But in reality such
diaries often served imperialist purposes. By devising a novel about
"mutual amity," Smith simply deflects attention from the harsh actu-
alities of history. Historian Peter Fryer (1988) summarizes that history:

> Most of the southern African communities were subjected by force:
> by scorched-earth campaigns meant to deprive the Africans of all
> means of independent livelihood. For these were not only land wars
> but also labour wars. Black people lost free access to the land, on
> which they were permitted to remain only as labourers, herdsmen,
> tenants or renters. (45)

As we examine another Dutch/African encounter, a story about the
"Great Trek" of 1836–1854, we again see varied tactics for appropri-
ating African land. Additionally, we find a continuing dissatisfaction
with the way British authorities handled land/labor policies, and we

find "race purity" as a strong motivating factor behind Dutch behavior. Maretha Maartens's *The Black Sheep* presents heroic trekboers and omits the realities of their military ventures and their racist ideology.

THE BLACK SHEEP

Maartens lets her very likeable hero, eleven-year-old Gideon, explain the reason for the trekking of his family in 1838:

> Adriaan [Gideon's guardian and older brother] sat waiting for better things: perhaps the English government at the Cape would see that the laws didn't work . . . perhaps they would give us money for gunpowder and muzzle-loaders . . . perhaps everything would be all right. Nothing was all right. . . . Only when nearly all the farmhouses in the district had been burnt down did Adriaan suddenly decide to leave Pa's farm to join the trek. . . . (7)

This is all the reader will hear about cause and effect, and it is presented from a trekker's perspective. Gideon's fictional trek coincides with the actual one led by Piet Retief, and the Retiefs left their own account for latter-day historians. Writing for the *Grahamstown Journal*, Retief explained the Boer grievances as (1) "turbulent and dishonest vagrants" (meaning the newly freed slaves the British had emancipated in 1833), (2) losses sustained when Boers were not recompensed adequately for their freed slaves, (3) "the plunder which we have endured from the Caffres and other coloured classes," and (4) the "odium which has been cast upon us . . . under the cloak of religion whose testimony is believed in England, to the exclusion of all evidence in our favour. . . ." (quoted in Thompson 1995, 69). (Retief is complaining here about the interference of the London Missionary Society.) Maartens's novel is so loaded with references to the trekboer's religious disposition that we can understand Retief's anger when his Godliness is impugned. His objection to the work of British missionaries, however, was directed at their abolitionism and complaints about Boer abuses of Blacks. These abuses included kidnapping and premeditated murder.

Another member of the Retief family, Piet's niece, wrote in her memoirs about her grievances regarding slave liberation; her objection was not with slave freedom but with their race per se:

> It is not so much their freedom that drove us to such lengths [to trek],
> as their being placed on equal footing with Christians, contrary to the
> laws of God and the natural distinction of race and religion, so that
> it was intolerable for any decent Christian to bow down beneath such
> a yoke; wherefore we rather withdrew in order thus to preserve our
> doctrines of purity. (quoted in Thompson 1995, 88)

The novelist first shows how the Boer's Black servants were loyal fellow trekkers, as seen when Gideon's sister-in-law is killed in a Zulu raid and her newborn is breast-fed by one of the surviving servants. But when Piet Retief is assassinated by Dingane (the successor of the renowned Zulu leader, Shaka), the reader is reminded about Black brutality, not Retief's racist views of Africans and his military campaigns against them. Retief had commented in his letter to the *Grahamstown Journal* that "we will uphold the just principles of liberty; but, whilst we will take care that no one shall be held in a state of slavery, it is our determination to maintain such regulations as may . . . preserve proper relations between master and servant" (quoted in Thompson 1995, 88). In short, he would not let the British catch them as slaveholders, but they would still sustain a *de facto* master/slave relationship.

According to the actual historical record, Retief had been negotiating with Dingane about a land deal that would allow Boer occupation between the Mzimvubu and Tugela Rivers. On previous occasions he had participated in Dutch–African conflicts in a strategy designed to give him control of African territory. But his death at the hands of the African chief is presented as a breach of trust by the Africans and an act of pure malice. The Dutch launch a punitive expedition, and this ill-advised action results in the death of nearly everyone in Gideon's group. Finally the Dutch military hero, Andries Pretorius, arrives with cannons, guns, and five hundred men. The actual toll in this next battle, fought at "Blood River," included an estimated 3,000 dead Zulus and not a single Boer casualty. Thompson (1995) calls this a classic example of "the superiority of controlled fire, by resolute men from a defensive position, over Africans armed with spears . . ." (91). Following Afrikaner tradition, the novelist treats this military success as a case of divine intervention on behalf of the Boers. As Andries Pretorius claimed, God had shown him the right place for the battle, and, in Gideon's words, he told the people: "God knows, you haven't come here to murder or be murdered but this country has to be made safe for you and your children" (66). Here the right to possess and dispossess is taken to be a European's divine right. That God could conceivably have a relationship with Africans is unthinkable from the Dutch perspective.

The Blood River battle gains its fictional momentum from the charms of Gideon, the kind-hearted, unwashed rascal who humbly calls himself "the Black Sheep." He is a psychologically credible character, and as the tale's narrator he brings perpetual liveliness to each unfolding episode. Through the perspective of this very genial child-commentator, the Boer community comes across as God-centered, neighborly, hard-working, and brave.

But the depiction of Africans is another matter. Although they are brave, they are also treacherous, cunning, faithless in treaty negotiations, and slayers of innocent women and children. As for the Black servants, it is implied that they were contented with their lot under racist "masters."

* *

In interpreting this history and its fictional presentation, we should note that the British and Dutch were not very far apart in their ideological stance vis-à-vis Africans. As much as the Dutch sought territorial and administrative autonomy (and as much as they were irked by the London Missionary Society), they could have found common ground with the English regarding subjugation of Blacks. Neither group wanted self-rule or civil rights for the Africans. The British governor, at the time of the Fish River boundary dispute, wrote in his report to his superiors in London:

> I am happy to add that in the course of this service there has not been shed more Kaffir blood than would seem to be necessary to impress on the minds of these savages a proper degree of terror and respect. (Thompson 1995, 55)

Unfortunately, much historical fiction for the young echoes this contempt, whether the storyteller is of British or Dutch descent.

WORKS CITED

Fryer, Peter. 1988. *Black People in the British Empire: An Introduction*. London: Pluto Press.

Maartens, Maretha. 1989. *The Black Sheep*. Pretoria, S.A.: Daan Retief Publishers.

Smith, Ken. 1987. *Tinde in the Mountains*. Johannesburg, S.A.: Ravan Press.

Thompson, Leonard. 1995. *A History of South Africa*. Revised edition. New Haven and London: Yale University Press.

NOTE

1. Ken Smith is a South African historian who, prior to this story for children, had already established himself as a writer of novels. As a fiction writer for adult readers, he has used different pseudonyms.

CHAPTER 10

Tales of Conquest and Religious Conversion

lack theology is not at odds with Christianity, according to Black South African martyr Steve Biko. Rather Black theology is at odds with the purposes for which Christianity has been put to use in South Africa. Christianity was brought into close alliance with colonization, and with an unholy war against the African people. In *The Great Thirst* (1971, 1985) and *The Hungry People* (1992), Jenny Seed lets missionary zeal on behalf of the Christian colonizers point the direction of each story.[1] Her overall approach is to choose a few African characters as her mouthpiece—characters who will act out the assumed validity of selected Biblical passages. Simultaneously she emphasizes the supposed backwardness of African culture in *The Great Thirst* and the sustaining power of the Bible during wartime in *The Hungry People*. The settings for these two stories are the African wars in the early 1820s and the Boer War campaign at Mafeking in 1900.

As we examine these books, we will elaborate upon the missionary presence in South Africa, a presence that Biko (1986) explains as integral to the imperialist enterprise. He writes:

> We can immediately see the logic of bringing in the missionaries to the forefront of the colonisation process. Whenever one succeeds in making a group of people accept a foreign concept in which he [in this case, the missionary] is an expert, he creates out of them perpetual students whose progress in the particular field can only be evaluated by him and on whom the student shall constantly rely for guidance and promotion. In being forced to accept the Anglo–Boer culture, the

blacks have allowed themselves to be at the mercy of the white
man. . . . (31–32)

With an unshakeable belief in the superiority of their own religious
tenets, the Anglo–Boer Christians would argue that theirs was a scientific religion, while Africans were mired in superstition. This is a classic example of first defining "knowledge," and then legitimizing it for
self-serving purposes. African American sociologist Patricia Hill
Collins (1998) writes: "Separating questions of what counts as knowledge from questions of who decides what knowledge is—in effect, sev-
ering epistemology from power—privileges elites" (xii). Collins alludes
to the general problem of consolidating power—of building hierarchies on an intellectual base—and this process is especially transparent
in South Africa. Under colonial rule and Apartheid the effects of a self-
aggrandizing "knowledge" system have been devastating. Anglo–Boer
claims to godliness were accompanied by horrendous acts of genocide
and dispossession.

By invoking the authority of self-selected Biblical passages, Seed
deflects attention from the South African record of human rights abuses. And when focusing on Black characters, she provides Biblical passages suggesting the nobility of submissiveness, the value of patience in
adversity, and the prudence of total subservience to the ruling authorities. This convenient misuse of Scripture is a contradiction of valid
"Christian ethics," but it legitimizes the historical path of colonial
invaders. This is not to dismiss the humanitarian work on the part of
missionary societies (which is also a part of the historical record), but
by perpetuating the white supremacy myth, the missionaries were
diminishing their potential for constructive action. *The Great Thirst*
takes the missionary side without illuminating the ironies in Christian
missionary history.

THE GREAT THIRST

This novel emphasizes an alleged self-destructiveness in Africans. It
posits a necessity for Western intervention as a means of stabilizing
crumbling indigenous societies. The Christian's pure benevolence is
placed in contrast to the degradation of "cunning little Bushmen,"
power-crazed tribal leaders, Black slave-catchers, and people wallow-
ing in "frenzies of madness."

Seed singles out one African child, Garib, to carry the Christian doctrine and make good the missionary's promise: "[We are here] to set free from sins," to "bring you out of darkness" (79). To make her point, the author creates an appalling level of "darkness," an unrelenting series of killings, tortures, and plunderings. This mayhem brings to mind Chinua Achebe's (1989) observation that in Western psychology there is an apparent need "to set Africa up as a foil to Europe, as a place of negations . . . in comparison with which Europe's own state of spiritual grace will be manifest" (2–3). Seed structures her story around this kind of polarity.

The story's setting is a drought that spurred migrations in the 1820s into what is now known as Namibia. The northerners, Hereros people, were successfully challenging the Khoikhois until a Khoikhoi kinsman, Jonker Afrikaner, arrived from the Cape Colony with horses, guns, White missionaries, and traders. He was a mixed race or "Coloured" African and has been called in history books "The Napoleon of the South." Seed begins her story when Garib is seven years old and takes him through battles, enslavement, a worshipful adoration of Jonker Afrikaner, and conversion to Afrikaner's Christian faith. The complex plot developments serve to teach Garib how wars breed more wars, and how the philosophical maxim of his people— "blood must pay with blood"—is a mistake.

In addition to the peace-over-war theme, the missionaries introduce Western cultural customs (Biblical names, frequent bathing, European garments). But as it turns out, such customs only exacerbate alleged African weaknesses. These include indolence, drunkenness, opium addiction, hedonism, and malicious trickery. Jonker Afrikaner, although a convert, is unable to maintain order, and he is seen as lacking the special mixture of self-discipline and material well-being that a Christian culture entails. Only Garib's pilgrimage is a success; that is, he abandons "an eye for an eye" philosophy, associates freedom with Christian purity, and gains an allegiance to the things of the spirit.

Ironically, Seed's book is espousing Christian peace while grossly sensationalizing descriptions of the non-Christian world. It would seem that only a Goliath-sized enemy is adequate to achieve the desired impression on young readers. But English professor Elwyn Jenkins (1993) writes approvingly that Seed's works "occupy an exceptional place in forming the historical sensibilities of white South Africans" (110). The sensibilities of indigenous South Africans is apparently not an issue. Steve Biko (1986) commented pessimistically that it would be "naive of us to expect our conquerors to write unbiased histories about us." Moreover, he abhorred the sensationalism in which Anglo-Boers indulged themselves: "Not only is there no objectivity in the history taught us but frequently there is an appalling misrepresentation of facts that is sickening even to the uninformed student" (32).

Jenny Seed fits Biko's profile of the miseducator, but she continues to be widely admired in White South African and Western circles. Her books have been published by British as well as South African publishers, and Jay Heale (1994) calls her "the mother of South African children's literature" (38). But she has come under stern criticism from American anthropologist Nancy Schmidt (1989), who writes that despite some sympathetic portrayals, such images in *The Great Thirst* are "overshadowed by negative stereotypes" (865).

In 1992 Seed was still following the familiar pattern of inserting Biblical passages in a story and letting them produce her theme. *The Hungry People* takes this approach as it centers on wartime and the need for Christian conversion.

THE HUNGRY PEOPLE

In depicting Whites battling Whites in the Boer War, Seed's approach is quite different from the one she employs when Blacks battle Blacks. Everyone in combat is Christian, everyone behaves in a civil manner, even when lobbing cannon balls at one another. When there is any surliness, meanness, or foolishness, it comes from the Barolongs, the African people residing on the outskirts of Mafeking. But most of the dramatic tension centers on a food shortage, since the town of Mafeking is under siege for 217 days and completely cut off from supply lines. The Barolong people are facing starvation, and the narrative concentrates on Barolong characters, especially fifteen-year-old Rojane. We see the war and civilian suffering from his vantage point.

Rojane's grandfather tells him the history of his people—how they were persecuted by the Matebeles and sought refuge with the English queen. Barolongs, such as those in his own family, moved to a Christian mission and learned "wisdom and faith from the Book" (40). Rojane's father became a teacher at the mission school, but is presently a letter carrier for the British army. When he is wounded, he seeks safety as a farm laborer on a Boer farm some distance from Mafeking's battle zone. His family does not know where he is or whether he is dead or alive. Thus Rojane feels the pressure of being the "man of the house" and caring for his mother, grandfather, baby sister, and disabled brother. He reads to the family from the Bible daily and ponders a text from Psalms: "There is a river, the streams whereof shall make glad the city of God" (29).

The reader can soon tell that this passage is sustaining the grandfather as he grows weaker and finally dies. Before his death he steals and slaughters a horse to bring food to his family, and this is a moral lapse that haunts grandfather mercilessly. Just before his last breath, he remembers that God forgives sinners and this gives him peace as he succumbs to malnutrition and old age. He also has a last minute chance to explain to his grandson the meaning of "the streams [that] make glad the city of God"—namely, that "there is a kind of gladness that comes from the All-Father, which no one can take from you" (43).

This optimistic idea sinks in very gradually, but ultimately the boy weeps over grandfather's heroic self-sacrifice and his deep trust in God. Rojane even becomes like grandfather as he turns his attention to the Biblical reassurances that served the old man so continuously. In the end, the real climax for the boy is not his father's safe return to the family or the end of the siege, but the realization that Christian dedication gives one the real victory.

This is one way an author can convey spiritual convictions to a reader, but this is not Seed's whole agenda. She does not simply leave Rojane with this newfound inspiration. Instead she makes her "glad city" text from Psalms serve the colonizer's needs. She shows how Rojane now lowers his career expectations and is altogether glad about doing so. Rojane realizes that under White rulers he will not be allowed to fulfill his aspirations and take the civil service exams. He will not be able to advance his prospects or his status within South African society. But that, apparently, is okay with him:

> Rojane took a few long, deep breaths. His mind was calm at last. . . .
> He closed his eyes. Tomorrow was the beginning of the future, he thought, whatever that might bring. Even if there might no longer be Civil Service Examinations for someone of the Barolong people, he could work to be a teacher like Father . . .
>
>   "There is a river, the streams whereof shall make glad the city of God." That verse that had once puzzled him came back like a gentle echo. . . . (93–94)

This story puts White and Black Christians side by side and asks Blacks to accept peaceably their subjugated condition under those same White Christians. But Black/White encounters under a Christian banner can be interpreted in quite a different way. Activist Allan Boesak (1986) pinpoints the dilemma for Black Christians:

> Black Theology is the theological reflection of black Christians on the situation in which they live and on their struggle for liberation. Blacks ask: What does it mean to believe in Jesus Christ when one is black and living in a world controlled by white racists? And what if these racists call themselves Christians also? (41)

These questions are not answered, but they signify, says Boesak, "a completely new phase in race relations in the world, a new psychological, social and political reality" (41).

This is the hopeful side. The negative side concerns childhood education. Steve Biko (1986) cautioned South Africans about the power of historical miseducation, about rigorous efforts to colonize the mind. He warned that "colonialism is never satisfied with having the native in its grip but, by some strange logic, it turns to his past and disfigures and distorts it" (32). The hope and the warning are both relevant to strategies leading to Boesak's "new phase in race relations."

WORKS CITED

Achebe, Chinua. 1989. *Hopes and Impediments: Selected Essays*. New York: Doubleday.

Biko, Steve. 1986. "Black Consciousness and the Quest for a True Humanity." In *One Day in June: Poetry and Prose from Troubled Times*, ed. Sisa Ndaba, 25–35. Rotterdam: Ad.Donker/Publisher.

Boesak, Allan. 1986. "Farewell to Innocence." In *One Day in June: Poetry and Prose from Troubled Times*, ed. Sisa Ndaba, 41. Rotterdam: Ad.Donker/Publisher.

Collins, Patricia Hill. 1998. *Fighting Words: Black Women and the Search for Justice*. Minneapolis and London: University of Minnesota Press.

Heale, Jay. 1994. *South African Authors & Illustrators.* Grabouw, S.A.: Bookchat.

Jenkins, Elwyn. 1993. *Children of the Sun: Selected Writers and Themes in South African Children's Literature.* Johannesburg: Ravan Press.

Schmidt, Nancy J. 1989. "Jenny Seed." In *Twentieth Century Children's Writers*, 3rd ed. ed. Tracy Chevalier, 864–866. Chicago and London: St. James Press.

Seed, Jenny. 1992. *The Hungry People.* Cape Town: Tafelberg Publishers.

Seed, Jenny. [1971, 1973] 1985. *The Great Thirst.* Revised edition. Cape Town: Tafelberg Publishers.

NOTE

1. Jenny Seed was educated at Ellerslie High School in Cape Town and now lives in Northdene, Natal. Her first book was published in 1964, and she has been a prolific writer for children since that time, being known especially for her historical fiction.

CONCLUSION

"Is This Going to Be a Democratic Society or Not?"

Poet Dennis Brutus posed this question in 1994 and concluded that it was still an open question—that South Africa needed the injection of "progressive ideas and progressive influences" if it was to better its chances for democratic change (Davies 1994, 103). The novels critiqued in this study represent, in our view, regression rather than progression. Apartheid is on the scene in these stories, but the novelists serve in varying degrees as apologists for this system. Is there any way that such a perspective can promote a democratic society?

A specific slant of the pen is what we have been trying to make plain. It is true that fiction is about character, not about encylopedic facts, but the characters interact with a total setting. The novelists in our sample explicitly introduce such aspects of the setting as the Forced Removal policy, the Prohibition of Mixed Marriages Act, the Group Areas Act, the 1994 Election Campaign, and other Apartheid-related events. When our literary critiques point to political and economic information, this is not to imply that the narrative should incorporate fact-laden material, but only that the novel should not distort it for white supremacist purposes. So how do the novelists cover the sociopolitical backgrounds they introduce? In a word, even in the post-1994 novels, Blacks are portrayed as essentially unready for self-rule.

The slant of the pro-Apartheid pen corresponds in large degree with Commissioner Wynand Malan's "Minority Report" in the Truth and Reconciliation Commission's Report of 1999. Many children's authors, like Malan (1999), seem to feel no clear need to criticize the country's recent repressive history. Malan, in fact, is aggrieved by the new government's critical stance. He objects to putting Apartheid on trial; he sees

Apartheid as being maligned by the Commission with "untested allega-
tions"; he sees the Commission as one-sided in relation to Communist
threats (to him, Communism is South Africa's human rights problem); he
sees conflicts of the past as unfairly politicized by the anti-Apartheid forces;
he sees those who were tortured by the police as unreliable witnesses (as
people who present exaggerated testimony or a biased perspective); he sees
National Party leaders as deserving more credit, and so on (440–443).

Why is children's literature so often representative of Malan's point of
view? This literature remains part of the larger educational system, one that
revolves around the myth that Africans on every level are backward, dysfunctional, and frequently dangerous. Storytellers sustain this overall
impression while making some gestures toward political change. In Dennis
Bailey's *Thatha*, for example, there is a Black electoral candidate, but he
represents dishonest campaign tactics, cunning demagoguery, and extreme
child abuse (incestuous rape). No mitigating images of the Black political
world are placed before the reader. In fact, worthy Black adults are con-
spicuously missing from the whole South African children's literature
canon. Adult Africans are either represented as fools, corrupting forces, or
hopeless failures.

Given the recurring anti-African messages, what are the prospects for a
"New" South Africa? Can the democratically elected leadership surmount
the ideological and structural hurdles?

THE IDEOLOGICAL BARRIER TO DEMOCRACY

We have suggested the scope of the white supremacist perspective throughout the larger Western world by quoting *favorable* American and British
reviews of books we find *unfavorable*. The removal of ideological barriers
is dependent upon their removal elsewhere in the world, yet South Africa
is a distinctive case.

The novelists in this study may have been indoctrinated in childhood
along the lines Robert Coles describes in *The Political Life of Children*
(1986). Coles found a deeply embedded conviction of white superiority in
his young White informants. One twelve-year-old Afrikaner told Coles:

> There is a lot of trouble with our black people. They are tribes . . . they
> fight tribal wars. We have tried to keep them from killing each other. They
> steal a lot and they cut one another up. . . . (187)

This boy told Coles that he feared Blacks throughout Africa: "There are millions of them. . . . They want to take away what we've got here. . . . We'll never let them. . . . Anyway, they wouldn't know what to do. They're not up to our level. . . . There's a big difference in intelligence" (188).

Another twelve-year-old (the son of a university professor) described for Coles his impression of "our black ones," our "Kaffirs":

> You know, they're different. They don't react the same way—they don't think the same way. There's a different metabolism. They're slower . . . I keep my distance; I have to, because I don't want to get sick! (197–198)

Coles sums up his twelve-year study with this conclusion: "Race rather than language or culture . . . is the true mainstay of nationalist sentiment. In the end, all white children of South Africa stare at black people, or at colored people, and invoke apartheid" (200).

Even some otherwise sympathetic White writers echo the convictions held by these children—namely, that Blacks are "not up to our [White] level." Thus the Black characters are positioned, at the end of the tale, in a low-status condition that is sometimes a slight improvement, but remains within the Apartheid-enforced boundaries.

Novelists who are critiqued in these pages may also have received their basic beliefs from South African textbooks. In the textbooks of the 1980s, historian Leonard Thompson (1985) found "no discernible increase in objectivity" (60). Professional South African historians were involved in this textbook enterprise, as Thompson explains. For example, Floris van Jaarsveld, "the most prolific and influential Afrikaner historian of his generation," is an ardent apologist for Apartheid. Thompson (1985) writes:

> [He] presented the *voortrekkers* as heroic figures whose "task was to tame the wilderness" and whose "only textbook was the Bible"; [he] used nineteenth-century history to imply that foreigners could not ever understand South Africa's problems; and [he] emphasized the dichotomy civilized-uncivilized. (60)

Another widely circulating history text "treats Blacks as natural subordinates of Whites." According to Thompson,

> [C. J. Joubert] vindicates the racial division of the labor force into well-paid, skilled, and relatively secure white workers and poorly paid, unskilled, and insecure black workers, without suggesting that it has had

anything to do with dispossession, taxation, curbs on black mobility, and pervasive discrimination. . . . (60)

Additionally, Joubert attributes any dissent among Africans to "international communism" (61). His perspective on the whole of tropical Africa is that the region suffers from Black backwardness and communist threats.

The total control of the school system has meant that this kind of indocrination could scarcely be avoided. When Commissioner Malan (1999) wrote his "Minority Report" for the TRC, he referred explicitly to his own early upbringing: "Choice," he said, "was not an option. I shared [the National Party's] history and its myths" (436). He continues:

> I supported Apartheid . . . as a moral option that I believed would lead away from domination and discrimination. . . . [In childhood] we were differently exposed and therefore differently disposed. . . . We represent . . . and empathise with [a number of different] value systems. (436)

While Malan tells of some viewpoint changes in the 1980s (for example, he began to see "elements of broader democratic choice"), he still sees himself as a victim—as a National Party leader who had no fair share in the Truth and Reconciliation proceedings. The TRC's report was, in his eyes, "railroaded" through by the Left. To read South African youth novels from 1985 to 1995 is to hear echoes of Malan's claim to victimhood. Novelists inevitably show either a White society under siege or a group of noble White paternalists making every effort to save Blacks from themselves.

The need for different teaching tools and different teachers seems clear enough, but the means to this end was not sufficiently prepared for in the negotiations leading to the 1994 elections. Structural changes did not go deep enough.

THE STRUCTURAL BARRIER TO DEMOCRACY

Where does education come in among the priorities of the post-Apartheid reconstruction? Who will be the architects who will design a system demanding full equality and integrating the future generations? African American sociologist James Turner (1983) has noted that "social justice itself is a structural question" (quoted in McWorter and Bailey 1983, 35). Put simply, the structural context within which a problem is generated must be understood if we are to know the meaning of a social issue. In his trial in 1963, Nelson Mandela emphasized the importance of education in the democratic struggle: "The present government has always sought to hamper Africans in their search for education . . ."; the secondary effects of this policy included "poverty and the breakdown of family life" (quoted in MacArthur 1992, 343–344).

The negotiators at the pre-1994 election conferences had much on their mind, including the drafting of an Interim Constitution that could ward off a major armed conflict. The fear of revolution abated, but a compromise was put into effect that penetrated every facet of the South African social structure. That is, people employed in the system could keep their jobs. Leonard Thompson (1995) writes:

> The new regime inherited a vast . . . public service of two million, dominated by male Afrikaners who were deployed in the administrative structures of the Apartheid state and its ten Homelands and many of whom had no sympathy for the goals of the Government of National Unity. . . . [T]he ANC had undertaken to guarantee the jobs and perquisites of all existing civil servants until they reached retirement age. (258)

This concession to the National Party was, says Thompson, "a major obstacle to the fulfillment of the goals of the new regime" (264). This structurally flawed compromise could only exacerbate the ideological problems.

The resulting educational mess has been one of the most intractable problems in post-1994 South Africa (e.g., in 1999 the national matriculation rate was only 48.9 percent). Children's literature can be identified as one branch of this problem. In this study we have referred to the prizes, bibliographies, academic studies, and other tools of the trade that have consistently rewarded pro-Apartheid books. This Eurocentric support apparatus is a continuing influence throughout the English-speaking world and beyond.

Overturning the longstanding structures of injustice is the new government's goal, but a complicating factor is the way justice was handled by the Truth and Reconciliation Commission. Although this Commission did incite the wrath of some National Party leaders (as in the case of Wynand Malan), it took a direction that left the perpetrators of the white supremacy myth and its cruelties untouched. Oddly enough, it was religious doctrine (a prominent element in the proceedings) that made the prospects for democracy more problematic.

MISDIRECTED RELIGIOSITY

South African historian T. R. H. Davenport (1998) notes that "change without a violent revolution did not seem possible in the 1980s" (3). Given this threat, it is perhaps understandable that Archbishop Desmond Tutu (1999), the chair of the TRC, used his religious principles and prestige for leverage in the post-1994 transition period. But his reconcilation-via-amnesty tactic has only complicated the problem of structuring justice in an even-handed manner.

The central question is whether or not one group's religious perspective should be allowed to override a largely neutral judicial process—a process based on widely acknowledged rules of evidence. Despite the looming threat to public order, is interference in the longstanding principles of adjudication an acceptable course of action? Is there really a great difference between the Afrikaners' claim that God appointed them to rule South Africa and the Commission's apparent assumption that it is God appointed as the dispenser of forgiveness to human rights violators?

In justifying the Commission's work, explanations given by Desmond Tutu (1999) seem contradictory. On the one hand he claims that the amnesty process arranged by the Commission is such an excellent process that "it assists in the cultivation of the new culture of respect for human rights." On the other hand he is denying the wisdom of any long-term amnesty policy:

> It is important to note, too, that the amnesty provision is an ad hoc arrangement meant for this specific purpose [encouraging accountability]. This is not how justice is to be administered in South Africa forever. It is for a limited and definite period and purpose. (54)

This seems to be saying in effect: "Let other people be connected with the rule of law but not us." If a waiver of the judicial process is for a limited time, then it seems misleading to call it the basis of "a new culture of respect for human rights." Finally, should the Archbishop be claiming that it was God's hand behind the political compromises of 1994? Tutu writes:

> Our experiment is going to succeed because God wants it to succeed, not for our glory and aggrandizement but for the sake of God's world. God wants to show that there is life after conflict and repression—that because of forgiveness there is a future. (282)

Historically, such personal claims to divine authority have been far too destructive to warrant repetition. Such claims lead to enormous leaps of self-justification. Yet this seemed to be an acceptable "out" for the Apartheid regime, and Tutu and the majority of Commissioners were in line with the "confess-and-repent" approach to truth finding. Unfortunately, the world at large offered few rebuttals, unlike its reaction to "ethnic cleansing" in the Balkans, Pinochet-led assassination practices, and other grave human rights cases.

What do we see as the educational ramifications of this amnesty policy? Is any retreat from the principles of judicial "due process" a valid precedent to lay before the young? Has "due process" not brought us as close to a method of truth finding as the human imagination has thus far been able to construct? Can the road to a "New South Africa" be successfully traveled if justice is abandoned as the prerequisite to peace and reconciliation? To what standards will the child at school be reconciled? What benefit or loss occurs if the meticulous procedures of the courtroom are honored or, contrariwise, disregarded? The logic of legal argument, the objectivity of examination and cross-examination—these are all missing when the TRC investigates but withholds a recommendation for legal action.

NEW PRESSURES/OLD MYTHS

Historian Mary Marshall Clark (2000) rightly sees the current South African story as much larger than itself. It is exposing widespread twentieth-century problems, and it is a case study for democracy itself. She looks at the "bloodless revolution," the transition after 1994, and the inequalities inherited from 350 years of White rule. She sees many global concerns teetering in the balance:

> If South Africa succeeds in addressing the complex inter-section of issues
> it faces, then the world will be more prepared to struggle with the issues
> of racism, sexism, nationalism, globalization, immigration, migration,
> underdevelopment, and ecological devastation, and more. (101)

This is a long list, and children are the people who will have this agenda passed down to them. In assessing the way youngsters are being prepared for this responsibility, we found many surprisingly blatant allusions to the "Black peril." Our study confirms what Grant Farrad (2000) sees in world opinion: namely, the presence of what he calls an "orientalist fantasy." This refers to the myth that Africa (like other non-Western civilizations) has an "excessive capacity for chaos" (62). After the ANC victories in the 1994 and 1999 elections, there sounded a hue and cry about "democracy in peril," about a "black planet" that would bury the tenets of liberal democracy. Constitutional "checks and balances" under the new regime would, some said, be tragically lost.

Similar doubts about Black self-rule recur in South African children's novels. In the books we examined, storytellers insinuated that a post-Apartheid government would likely fail, given Black primitivism (*The Witch Woman of the Hogsback*), urban self-destructiveness (*The Slayer of Shadows* and *The Ink Bird*), traitorous leadership (*The Day of the Kugel*), election fraud (*Thatha* and *Outside the Walls*) and nationalist-inspired separatism (*Skindeep*), to mention just a few examples.

Such assumptions are not confined to the children's book field. Western journalists often start with predictions of Black failure. For example, prior to the 1999 election, journalist Corrina Schuler (1999b) wrote: "Is South Africa poised to become next in the line of one-Party dictatorships on this [African] continent?" (1). In another report she slants her journalistic pen: "When it comes to Party politics, Mbeki's reputation as a ruthless operator remains unchanged" (1999a, 12). Throughout her report Schuler casts doubts upon Mandela's successor (e.g., "Analysts agree there has been a deliberate effort to soften his personality. . . . He has taken to . . . embracing supporters and dancing with a children's choir . . . ." [12]). Moreover, Schuler gives considerable space to those who charge Mbeki with ignoring competency in making appointments and selecting political lackeys (12). Given such a pessimistic standpoint, one wonders whether Western nations will come to South Africa's aid at this time of economic challenge. With 5 percent of the population owning 88 percent of the social wealth, the needed monetary redistribution seems almost beyond hope. In terms of the plight of children, this means that currently "less than 10 percent of school-leavers can expect to find regular work" (Murray 2000, 41). In Soweto, "70 percent of the sixteen- to twenty-five-year-olds not enrolled in school [are] unemployed" (Murray 2000, 41). This *suitably* employable group remains out of work, while the *unsuitable* (children ten to fourteen years of age) are working. Child labor is stemming the tide of devastating family poverty. In 1996, these children numbered 63,000 (47).

* *

Among the ironies of history is the way *children* played a leading part in bringing political change to South Africa, while children's *literature* remains one of the most regressive in the world. It constitutes an endless set of variations on the legitimacy of Apartheid. Africans (as we have noted throughout this book) are the "objects" that work the farms, mine the gold, cook the food, clean the house, wash the clothes, and nurse the children. They are presented as if their entire life's function is properly determined by the needs of White society.

The children of Soweto and elsewhere went to battle over this. They did not have the armoured weaponry of the Apartheid regime, but they knew they must demand their rights of citizenship, rights that had been denied to the generations that preceded them. When the school riots began in 1976, the killing of so many unarmed children sent shock waves around the world. Yet the children's writers have said very little about why these children had to abandon school, and why they sometimes lost their lives. Children's writers give the impression that this uprising was largely due to criminal or communist influences.

The rebellious young people had it right; they were following in the path of a long and honorable human rights tradition:

> "Give us free!" said Sengbe Pieh (leader of the Amistad Slave Revolt in 1839).
>
> "Free at last!" said Martin Luther King, Jr. (as he rallied Americans for civil rights in the 1960s).
>
> "Our march to freedom is irreversible" said Nelson Mandela (upon his release from prison in 1990).

WORKS CITED

Clark, Mary Marshall. 2000. "Judging the New South Africa." *Souls: A Critical Journal of Black Politics, Culture, and Society* 2, 2: 97–202.

Coles, Robert. 1986. *The Political Life of Children*. Boston, New York: The Atlantic Monthly Press.

Davenport, T. R. H. 1998. *The Transfer of Power in South Africa*. Cape Town: David Philip Publishers.

Davies, Geoffrey W. and Holger G. Ehling. 1994. "On a Knife Edge: Interview with Dennis Brutus." *Matatu* 11: 101–110.

Farrad, Grant. 2000. "Better the Devil You Know? The Politics of Colouredness and Post-Apartheid South African Elections in the Western Cape." *Souls: A Critical Journal of Black Politics, Culture, and Society* 2, 2: 50–64.

MacArthur, Brian, ed. 1992. "Nelson Mandela." In *Twentieth Century Speeches*, 468–470. New York: Penguin Books.

Malan, Wynarnd. 1999. "Minority Report," Vol. 5. *Truth and Reconciliation Commission of South Africa Report.* Vol. 1–5. London: Macmillan Reference Ltd., New York: Grove's Dictionaries.

McWorter, Gerald A. and Ronald W. Bailey. 1983. *Black Studies Curriculum Development in the 1980s: Patterns of Consensus, Conflict, and Change.* Afro Scholar Working Papers. Urbana: University of Illinois.

Murray, Martin J. 2000. "The New Winners and New Losers in South Africa After Apartheid." *Souls: A Critical Journal of Black Politics, Culture, and Society* 2, 2: 40–49.

Schuler, Corrina. 1999a. "After Legendary Mandela, Thabo Who?" *Christian Science Monitor* (June 1): 12–13.

Schuler, Corrina. 1999b. "Election Tips S. Africa Toward One-Party Rule." *Christian Science Monitor* (June 4): 1, 8.

Thompson, Leonard. 1985. *The Political Mythology of Apartheid.* New Haven and London: Yale University Press.

Tutu, Desmond Mpilo. 1999. *No Future Without Forgiveness.* New York: Doubleday.

The Anti-Apartheid Voices of Karen Press and Beverley Naidoo

[T]he artist's capacity to surprise and enrich an audience—by offering them an interpretation, a re-telling, a celebration of their reality that they *could not have asked for in advance*—is a great part of what makes art valuable to people. And this capacity is in no way contradictory to the idea of art as progressive, politically conscious or socially responsible.

The anti-Apartheid, anti-racist works of Karen Press[1] and Beverley Naidoo[2] became possible only after Mandela's release from prison, or from a location in exile. The state banned writings that were in opposition to itself, and when the 1994 election altered the state apparatus, the mentality of Apartheid remained difficult to reform since longstanding institutions were kept intact. In fact, the white supremacy myth is difficult to dislodge in many parts of the world, and in a consistently colonialist nation such as South Africa, the task is truly awesome. To sustain its political and economic control, the Apartheid regime had to exercise a deep and broad domination over South African culture, and this baneful tapestry must now be undone strand by strand. Models of democratic, non-racist literature become all the more significant in this environment, and Press's *Let It Come Back* (1992) and Naidoo's *Chain of Fire* (published first in Great Britain in 1989) are exceptional models. For the first time in South African literary history, Black children have been given a literature geared for them and rooted in their own historical experience.[3]

KAREN PRESS

Let It Come Back is Press's straightforward, unsentimental novel about township life under Apartheid. It is far removed from the self-condemning imagery presented in the township novels critiqued in this study. It is about the ghetto as neighborhood, as a boy's home ground where he lives out ordinary childhood pleasures and challenges. It's a terrain over which he has some degree of mastery, but this does not mean that Press underplays or underestimates the horrors of South African oppression. Rather the hardships of township life are intricately interwoven with a range of psychologically plausible characterizations.

In particular, twelve-year-old Mayibuye is delineated with a sure hand. His homelife has made it near to impossible to become well-acquainted with his father, and this unnatural condition produces an obsession in the boy after his father dies in a fatal car accident. Mayibuye will not accept any action that interferes with his stewardship of a box of mementoes placed in his hands by his father, even though he does not know the contents of the box. When the police confiscate this treasure during a routine midnight raid on his home, the plot is set in motion—a scenario in which Mayibuye will have difficult encounters with the authorities, with his mother, and with his schoolmates. As the story spins out, Mayibuye weighs all the conflicting interests and tries to mend all the torn relationships, while still remaining determined to fulfill his promise to his father to protect and cherish the contents of the box.

In the conclusion we learn that the father's legacy is only a clay ox figurine, a few corn stalks, a map of his kraal's location, and a photo of a graveyard, but the boy comes to understand their powerful symbolic meaning. He understands that his father's absence from his life (his father's watchman's job kept him at work from roughly 4 A.M. to 9 P.M.) was not his father's choice. In the end, a visit to his father's rural home and the rescue of three starving rural children brings together in Mayibuye's mind the visionary past and the stark present. He will help these young relatives survive in his own tough township world, and he will keep moving even in this unjust and unstable nation-state.

Without becoming preachy, Press brings to the foreground some important realities. She shows that under the Apartheid government, rural South Africa has been decimated, civil rights have been abolished, law has become a mockery, and economic deprivation has plagued the vast majority of people. Given these colonialist conditions, Mayibuye and his family are not about to make a false peace with even the most outwardly friendly police officers. When a constable argues that he is only a person like other persons, Mayibuye informs him that a "person" does not raid a family's home, steal their possessions, and assault their dignity. In a word, reconciliation must be rightly earned.

As an insider, Karen Press is able to make this novel work artistically. But it is important to add that she is an active cultural/political theorist in South Africa, and in her works she is putting into practice her well-reasoned ideals. Her abstractions about art and politics offer the children's book field an excellent theoretical map for the future.

Press's seminar paper at the Center for African Studies in 1990 lays out her credo. She discusses surprise, responsibility, and power as they relate to practicing artists within the liberation struggle. The people's war against Apartheid, racism, and white supremacy is a "given," not a debatable component in her philosophy. The overarching theme in her seminar paper revolves around how artistry and political justice interact: from the artist's perspective, there needs to be "an invitation to the artists to surprise their audiences" (1990). Press sees this invitation as a freedom to handle subjects from the artist's "*own* understanding, style and skills," and a freedom to receive direct feedback from audiences (1990, 70). In short, art is "too big" for rigid rules or for manipulation by even well-meaning intermediaries.

Social responsibility, however, is closely related to this creative freedom. Freedom to produce, Press says, is connected with the freedom to take responsibility for what one produces for the public. That includes a responsibility to *understand* (in the Apartheid context) the struggle for justice. It means accepting that whatever is produced "will have political significance," or otherwise it may well lack relevance in people's lives (1990, 70). It means that artists accept the challenge to develop their own aesthetic vocabulary; they do not merely gripe about the clichés that they associate with their more pedestrian comrades.

Press's tenets point to "new spaces" in a democratic South Africa— to a climate in which the ties between art and politics are understood in all their complexity. Government needs to supply the support systems that cultural activity often requires, but the creative spirit is not to be driven into exile, either literally or figuratively.[4]

BEVERLEY NAIDOO

Creating art in exile means creating it outside the very sources that nourish it. Thus Beverley Naidoo's *Chain of Fire* was not an easy project. This novel had to achieve a degree of closeness with South African realities, despite the author's exiled existence in Britain. One way to measure the novelist's success is to note how faithful the narrative is to the lived experiences chronicled in biographies and autobiographies by liberation leaders. In our view, Naidoo passes this test. In particular, she is faithful to what anti-Apartheid activists experienced in prison, in banishment, in the workplace, and in forced removals to barren "Homelands." Naidoo takes one ordinary Black family and lets their decisions and sufferings come to the reader as a coherent story.

Naledi, Tiro, and Dineo are child characters first introduced in 1984 in Naidoo's banned novel, *Journey to Jo'Burg*.⁵ In *Chain of Fire* Naidoo develops their family history at the point when so-called Black Spots are being removed by the South African government. That is, enclaves of Black residents are being moved to a "Homeland" arbitrarily designated as their "nation," their only place of "citizenship." Driven by the white supremacy myth and by simple "land-grabbing" expediency, this policy makes no provision for the lives it will disrupt. The children and their grandmother suddenly find themselves transported to intolerable conditions in Bophuthatswana.

The novel centers on the period leading to this deportation and fifteen-year-old Naledi's first efforts in anti-Apartheid resistance. In *Journey to Jo'Burg* Naledi had learned indirectly about Soweto's resistance movement, but now she must choose this hard path for herself. She has a mentor, a neighbor who has spent ten years imprisoned on Robben Island and is now living in banishment in her town. His courage inspires his own son, as well as Naledi and others, to join a secret school committee and lead a protest march against the forced removal. Both the march and the police crackdown give Naidoo an opportunity to say something about banishment, torture, assassination, and detention under the "Terrorism Act," and deprivation of food and water as forms of political pressure. As for legal redress, the petitions and meetings organized by the townsfolk are meaningless gestures, since the people's whole existence (whether in townships or "Homelands") is subsumed under the policy of expediently herding Black laborers.

Such content is woven unobtrusively into the novel as it relates to the daily living of nearly all Black South Africans; to chronicle a life in this nation is to automatically chronicle a series of injustices. Daily, commonplace routines are completely integrated with the edicts and actions of the police state authorities. The artistic challenge is to avoid abstractionism, to find instead a way to express concrete existence and become so close to the lived experiences that the story tells itself. Naidoo cites some sources within the novel that tend to have that effect—that connect the writer with very intimate details about the way that bureaucratic domination impinges upon routine, daily living (for example, she refers to *The Surplus People* by Laurine Platzky and

Cheryl Walker). In general, we see Naidoo practicing Press's philosophy: she blends her own creative freedom with a well-grounded understanding of political, social, and economic conditions and an unabashed social responsibility.

* *

South African poet Mongane Wally Serote (1990) has pinpointed the two alternatives for writers within an oppressed and exploited group. Either they will "engage in a struggle for the creation of a liveable world and future" (107) or, contrariwise, they will accommodate the oppressors and suffer alienation from the people. For his own part, he has tried to become "part and parcel of the energy that will create a liveable world" (109), and we see a similar aspiration behind the works of Press and Naidoo. They have shared the lives of the people they know and understand the size and depth of their subjugation.

But what about the "good" writers who are reactionary? This study has been about novels that are widely viewed by White book specialists as good books but that we find regressive. Their reactionism lies in their support of Apartheid and the white supremacy myth in general. Do the untruths of Apartheid diminish their artistry? Can any art that presumes to illuminate the human condition embrace such a pernicious mythology? On this point we think Serote's conclusions are relevant. He writes: "Racists . . . [can] be good writers for racists, if one measures their ability to spin out words and express ideas, even about racism. But good writing should be writing that makes the world a liveable place" (120). In the South African context, "liveable" has exceptionally deep connotations, since the lives and the life chances of so many have been lost.

WORKS CITED

Naidoo, Beverley. [1989, 1990] 1993. *Chain of Fire*. Illustrated by Eric Velasquez. Reprint, New York: Harper Trophy Edition (paperback).

Naidoo, Beverley. [1984] 1985. *Journey to Jo'Burg: A South African Story*. Reprint, New York: J. B. Lippincott (American edition illustrated by Eric Velasquez).

Press, Karen. 1992. *Let It Come Back*. Pietermaritzburg, S.A.: Centaur Publications (Pty) Ltd.

Press, Karen. 1990. "Surprise, Responsibility and Power." In *Spring Is Rebellious: Arguments About Cultural Freedom, by Abie Sacks and Respondents*, eds. Ingrid de Kok and Karen Press, 68–73. Cape Town: Buchu Books.

Serote, Mongane Wally. 1990. "The Role of Culture in the African Revolution: Ngugi wa Thiong'o and Mongane Wally Serote in a Roundtable Discussion." In *On the Horizon*, 105–126. Fordsburg, S.A.: The Congress of South African Writers.

NOTES

1. Karen Press is a superb poet, cultural theorist, non-profit publisher, and novelist for both children and adults. Her poems are collected in *Bird Heart Stoning the Sea* (1990), which also includes two short novels, *Krotoa's Story* and *Lines of Force, a Small Murder Mystery*. She is the coordinator of the publishing project "Buchu Books Open Door Publications" in Cape Town. This enterprise seeks out new writers and uses all profits in support of additional new works.

2. Beverley Naidoo was born in Johannesburg in 1943. At the age of twenty-one she was detained without trial, and subsequently lived in exile, working as a primary and secondary school teacher in London. In 1985 she published *Censoring Reality*, a study of nonfiction books which revealed the way Apartheid and racism were glossed over or even "dressed up to look positively good." She called this study a springboard indicating "how racism is still being condoned, and indeed promoted, through what is passing for 'educational media' in [Britain]" (*Censoring Reality*, ILEA Centre for Anti-Racist Education and the British Defence/Aid Fund for Southern Africa).

3. Parts of Peter Abraham's autobiographical novel, *Tell Freedom*, also give Black children an authentic account of their childhood experience in South Africa, but this book was not published as a children's book. A school edition of "Book One," however, was edited by W. G. Bebbington in 1963 and published by George Allen and Unwin in London. Abrahams had moved to Britain in the early 1940s.

4. For an expanded treatment of Karen Press's aesthetic and political philosophy, see her doctoral dissertation: "Towards a Revolutionary Artistic

Practice in South Africa," published by the Centre for African Studies, University of Cape Town, 1990.

5. *Journey to Jo'Burg* has been criticized as lacking character development, but this short "easy reader" is intentionally brief, being part of the "Knockout" series created for children with underdeveloped reading skills. Even with its generic limitations, the narrative possesses its own truth and opens up the realities of Apartheid for young readers.

Selected Bibliography

SOCIAL/POLITICAL STUDIES

Biko, Steve. *I Write What I Like*. London: Heinemann Education Books, Ltd., 1987. (Originally published in 1978).

Callinicos, Alex. *South Africa Between Reform and Revolution*. London, Chicago, Melbourne: Bookmarks, 1988.

Davenport, T. R. H. *The Transfer of Power in South Africa*. Cape Town: David Philip Publishers, 1998.

Davidson, Basil. "Africa Recolonized?" In *Amistad 2*, eds. John A. Williams and Charles F. Harris. New York: Vintage Books, 1971.

Dubow, Saul. *Scientific Racism in Modern South Africa*. Cambridge: Cambridge University Press, 1995.

Frankel, Philip, Noam Pines, and Mark Swelling, eds. *State, Resistance and Change in South Africa*. London, New York, Sydney: Croom Helm, 1988.

Fredrickson, George M. *Black Liberation: A Comparative History of Black Ideologies in the United States and South Africa*. New York and Oxford: Oxford University Press, 1995.

Fredrickson, George M. *White Supremacy: A Comparative Study in American and South African History*. New York and Oxford: Oxford University Press, 1981.

Fryer, Peter. *Black People in the British Empire: An Introduction*. London: Pluto Press, 1988.

Hanlon, J. *Beggar Your Neighbours: Apartheid Power in South Africa*. Bloomington: Indiana University Press; London: James Currey Press, 1986.

Harrison, Nancy. *Winnie Mandela: Mother of a Nation*. London: Victor Gollancz Ltd., 1985.

Hirson, Baruch. *Year of Fire, Year of Ash: The Soweto Revolt: Roots of a Revolution?* London: Zed Press, 1979.

Howarth, David R. and Aletta J. Norval. *South Africa in Transition: New Theoretical Perspectives*. London: Macmillan Press Ltd.; New York: St. Martin's Press, 1998.

Iliffe, John. *Africans: The History of a Continent*. Cambridge: Cambridge University Press, 1995.

Kitchen, Helen and J. Coleman Kitchen, eds. *South Africa: Twelve Perspectives on the Transition*. Westport, CT: Praeger, 1994.

Leach, Graham. *South Africa: No Easy Path to Peace*. Rev. ed. London: Methuen, 1987.

Le May, G. H. L. *The Afrikaners: An Historical Interpretation*. Oxford: Blackwell Publishers, 1994.

MacDonald, Michael. "Power Politics in the New South Africa." *Journal of Southern African Studies*, 22:2 (June 1996): 221–233.

Magubane, Bernard Makhosezwe. *The Political Economy of Race and Class in South Africa*. New York and London: Monthly Review Press, 1979, 1990.

Mandela, Nelson. *Long Walk to Freedom: The Autobiography of Nelson Mandela*. Boston, New York, and London: Little, Brown and Co., 1994; Back Bay Books, 1995.

Marks, Shula and Stanley Trapido, eds. *The Politics of Race, Class and Nationalism in Twentieth Century South Africa*. London and New York: Longman Group, 1987.

Marx, Anthony W. *Lessons of Struggle: South African Internal Opposition, 1960–1990*. New York and Oxford: Oxford University Press, 1992.

Marx, Anthony W. *Making Race and Nation: A Comparison of South Africa, The United States, and Brazil.* Cambridge: Cambridge University Press, 1998.

Mermelstein, David, ed. *The Anti-Apartheid Reader: The Struggle Against White Racist Rule in South Africa.* New York: Grove Press, 1987.

Murray, Nancy. "Somewhere Over the Rainbow: A Journey to the New South Africa." *Race and Class*, 38:3 (1997): 1–24.

Ngeokovane, Cecil. *Demons of Apartheid: A Moral and Ethical Analysis of the N.G.K., N.P. and Broederbond's Justification of Apartheid.* Cape Town and Johannesburg: Skotaville Publishers, 1989.

Norval, Aletta J. *Deconstructing Apartheid Discourse.* London and New York: Verso, 1996.

Pampallis, John. *Foundations of the New South Africa.* London and Atlantic Highlands, NJ: Zed Books; Cape Town: Maskew Miller Longman, 1991.

Platzky, Laurine and Cheryl Walker. *The Surplus People: Forced Removals in South Africa.* Johannesburg: Ravan Press, 1985.

Schutte, Gerhard. *What Racists Believe: Race Relations in South Africa and the United States.* Thousand Oaks, CA, London, and New Delhi: Sage Publications, 1995.

Souls: A Critical Journal of Black Politics, Culture, and Society, 2:2 (Spring 2000). This issue focuses exclusively on South Africa.

Thompson, Leonard. *A History of South Africa.* Rev. ed. New Haven and London: Yale University Press, 1995.

Thompson, Leonard. *The Political Mythology of Apartheid.* New Haven and London: Yale University Press, 1985.

Toase, F. H. and E. J. Yorke. *The New South Africa: Prospects for Domestic and International Security.* London: Macmillan Press Ltd.; New York: St. Martin's Press, 1998.

Truth and Reconciliation Commission. *Truth and Reconciliation Commission of South Africa Report*, Vol. 1–5. London: Macmillan Reference Ltd.; New York: Grove's Dictionaries Inc., 1999.

Tsotsi, W. M. *From Chattel to Wage Slavery: A New Approach to South African History*. Maseru, Lesotho: Lesotho Printing and Publishing Co., 1981, 1985.

Unterhalter, Elaine. *Forced Removal: The Division, Segregation and Control of the People of South Africa*. London: International Defence and Aid Fund for Southern Africa, 1987.

Waldmeir, Patti. *Anatomy of a Miracle: The End of Apartheid and the Birth of the New South Africa*. New York and London: W. W. Norton and Co., 1997.

Woods, Donald. *Apartheid: The Propaganda and the Reality*. London: International Affairs Div., Commonwealth Secretariat, 1985.

Worden, Nigel. *The Making of Modern South Africa*. Second ed. Oxford, UK: Blackwell Publishers, 1995.

LITERARY STUDIES

Achebe, Chinua. *Hopes and Impediments: Selected Essays*. New York and London: Doubleday, 1989.

Ahmad, Aijaz. "The Politics of Literary Postcoloniality." *Race and Class*, 36:3 (1995): 1–20.

Boehmer, Elleke, Laura Chrisman, and Kenneth Parker, eds. *Altered State? Writing and South Africa*. Sydney, Australia, Mundelstrup, Denmark, and West Yorkshire, UK: Dangaroo Press, 1994.

Clayton, Cherry, ed. *Women and Writing in South Africa: A Critical Anthology*. London: Heinemann, 1989.

Dabydeen, David, ed. *The Black Presence in English Literature*. Manchester: Manchester University Press, 1985.

Davis, Geoffrey and Holger G. Ehling. "On a Knife Edge: Interview with Dennis Brutus." *Matatu* 11, 1994.

February, V. A. *Mind Your Colour: The "Coloured" Stereotype in South African Literature.* London and Boston: Kegan Paul Pub., 1981.

Hammond, Dorothy and Alta Jablow. *The Africa That Never Was.* New York: Twayne Publishers, 1970.

Katz, Wendy R. *Rider Haggard and the Fiction of Empire: A Critical Study of British Imperial Fiction.* New York: Cambridge University Press, 1987.

Killam, G. D. *Africa in English Fiction, 1874–1939.* Ibadan, Nigeria: Ibadan University Press, 1968.

Morrison, Toni. *Playing in the Dark: Whiteness and the Literary Imagination.* Cambridge, MA: Harvard University Press, 1992; New York: Vintage Books, 1993.

Nuttall, Sarah and Carli Coetzee. *Negotiating the Past: The Making of Memory in South Africa.* New York, Oxford, and Cape Town: Oxford University Press, 1998.

Ogbaa, Kalu. "An Interview with Chinua Achebe." *Research in African Literatures* 12:1 (Spring 1981): 1–13.

Peck, Richard. *A Morbid Fascination: White Prose and Politics in Apartheid South Africa.* Westport, CT and London: Greenwood Press, 1997.

Press, Karen. *Towards a Revolutionary Artistic Practice in South Africa.* Cape Town: Centre for African Studies, University of Cape Town, 1990.

Serote, Mongane Wally. *On the Horizon.* Fordsburg, S.A.: The Congress of South African Writers, 1990.

Sheckels, Jr., Theodore F. *The Lion on the Freeway: A Thematic Introduction to Contemporary South African Literature in English.* New York, Bern, Berlin: Peter Lang, 1996.

Trump, Martin, ed. *Rendering Things Visible: Essays on South African Literary Culture.* Johannesburg: Ravan Press, 1990.

CHILDHOOD STUDIES: POLITICAL AND LITERARY[1]

Burman, Sandra and Pamela Reynolds, eds. *Growing Up in a Divided Society: The Contexts of Childhood in South Africa.* Johannesburg: Ravan; Oxford: The Centre for Cross-Cultural Research on Women, Oxford University, 1986.

Castle, Kathryn. *Britannia's Children: Reading Colonialism through Children's Books and Magazines.* Manchester and New York: Manchester University Press, 1996.

Coles, Robert. *The Political Life of Children.* Boston and New York: The Atlantic Monthly Press, 1986.

"Education in South Africa: Five Personal Accounts." *Interracial Books for Children Bulletin,* 16:5 and 6 (1985): 16–21.

Everatt, David, ed. *Creating a Future: Youth Policy for South Africa.* Johannesburg: Ravan Press, 1994. (Produced for the Joint Enrichment Project [JEP] and for CASE: the Community Agency for Social Enquiry.)

Guy, Arnold. *Held Fast for England: G.A. Henty, Imperialist Boys' Writer.* London: Hamish Hamilton, 1980.

Jones, Sean. *Assaulting Childhood: Children's Experiences of Migrancy and Hostel Life in South Africa.* Johannesburg: Witwatersrand University Press, 1993.

Khorana, Meena. "Apartheid in South African Children's Fiction." *Children's Literature Association Quarterly,* 13:2 (1988): 52–56.

Khorana, Meena, ed. *Critical Perspectives on Postcolonial African Children's and Young Adult Literature.* Westport, CT, and London: Greenwood Press, 1998.

Logan, Mawuena Kossi. *Narrating Africa: George A. Henty and the Fiction of Empire.* New York and London: Garland Publishing, 1999.

Logan, Mawuena. "Pushing the Imperial/Colonial Agenda: G.A. Henty's *The Young Colonists.*" *Journal of African Children's and Youth Literature,* 6 (1994/95).

"Long Struggle for Change." (Brief biographies of South African liberationists.) *Interracial Books for Children Bulletin,* 16:5 and 6 (1985): 22–27.

Maddy, Yulisa Amadu and Donnarae MacCann. *African Images in Juvenile Literature: Commentaries on Neocolonialist Fiction.* Jefferson, NC: McFarland and Co., 1996.

MacCann, Donnarae. *White Supremacy in Children's Literature: Characterizations of African Americans, 1830–1900.* New York and London: Garland Publishing (The Taylor & Francis Group), 1998. (Paperback edition : Routledge, 2001.)

Maddy, Yulisa Amadu and Donnarae MacCann. "Ambivalent Signals in South African Young Adult Novels." *Bookbird: World of Children's Books,* 36:1 (Spring 1998): 27–32.

Reynolds, Pamela. *Childhood in Crossroads: Cognition and Society in South Africa.* Cape Town and Johannesburg: David Philip; Grand Rapids, MI: Wm. B. Eerdmans, 1989.

Seekings, Jeremy. *Heroes or Villains? Youth Politics in the 1980s.* Johannesburg: Ravan Press, 1993. (Researched and written for the Joint Enrichment Project by the Community Agency for Social Enquiry.)

NOTE

1. Books that we have excluded from listing in this section include works that we severely criticize throughout this book. For example, Elwyn Jenkins's *Children of the Sun: Selected Writers and Themes in South African Children's Literature* (Johannesburg: Ravan Press, 1993); Jay Heale's *From the Bushveld to Biko: The Growth of South African Children's Literature in English from 1907 to 1992 Traced through 110 Notable Books* (Grabouw, S.A.: Bookchat, 1996); Jay Heale's *South African Authors & Illustrators* (Grabouw, S.A.: Bookchat, 1994); Shirley Davies's *Reading Roundabout: A Review of South African Children's Literature* (Pietermaritzburg, S.A.: Shuter & Shooter, 1992).

Index